Hymns–

How to Sing Them

Edited by

Mandus A. Egge

and

Janet Moede

Prepared under the auspices

of

The Commission on Worship and Church Music

The American Lutheran Church

AUGSBURG PUBLISHING HOUSE

Minneapolis, Minnesota

HYMNS — HOW TO SING THEM

THANK YOU

to Mr. Harold Belgum, Pastor Thomas Herbranson, Mr. Vernon Knutson, Mr. Ronald A. Nelson, and Mr. Mayo Savold who prepared the design and format of this book.

THANK YOU

to the editorial committee, Pastor Thomas Herbranson, Mr. Vernon Knutson, Mrs. Norman Moen, and Mr. Ronald A. Nelson, who with the editors continued the work and prepared the materials for publication.

THANK YOU

to those who prepared the chapters in this book, whose work is truly a labor of love. It is our hope that the suggestions given will help make Lutheran congregations truly singing congregations.

THANK YOU

to all who contributed their suggestions for introducing and teaching the hymns in the Hymn of the Week series.

THANK YOU

to Dr. O. G. Malmin and Miss Ruth Olson of Augsburg Publishing House for valuable suggestions and for assistance in preparing the manuscript, and to the Division of Parish Education of The American Lutheran Church for encouragement and assistance in preparing the material.

THE EDITORS

CONTENTS

Part I

1. Introducing Hymns—How to Sing Them 3
   MANDUS A. EGGE

2. Getting Families to Sing at Home 6
   HAROLD J. BELGUM

3. Teaching Hymns to Pre-Reading Children 8
   BETTY ANN RAMSETH

4. Teaching Hymns to Primary Children 10
   MARTI WILSON

5. Teaching Hymns to Juniors 13
   RONALD A. NELSON

6. Teaching Hymns to Confirmands and Adults 16
   THOMAS E. HERBRANSON

7. Congregational Hymn Rehearsals 19
   KATHRYN ULVILDEN MOEN

8. Use of Instruments with Hymn Singing 22
   VERNON C. KNUTSON

9. Hymn Festivals 25
   KATHRYN ULVILDEN MOEN

Part II

SUNDAY	SBH NO.	HYMN	PAGE
Advent I	11	O how shall I receive thee	31
Advent II	8	Lift up your heads, ye mighty gates	32
Advent III	12	Comfort, comfort ye, my people	33
Advent IV	2	O come, O come, Emmanuel	34
Christmas	22	From heaven above to earth I come	36
Christmas I	21	All praise to thee, Eternal Lord	37
Christmas II	281	Let all mortal flesh keep silence	38
Epiphany	404	How brightly beams the morning star	39
Epiphany I	17	Of the Father's love begotten	40
Epiphany II	572	Children of the heavenly Father	41

SUNDAY	SBH NO.	HYMN	PAGE
Epiphany III	307	Jesus shall reign	42
Epiphany IV	212	Come, thou bright and morning star	44
Epiphany V	257	God's word is our great heritage	45
Septuagesima	372	Out of the depths I cry to thee	46
Sexagesima	250	O God of Light	47
Quinquagesima	58	Alleluia, song of sweetness	48
Lent I	65	My song is love unknown	49
Lent II	85	Ah, holy Jesus	51
Lent III	67	Jesus, Name all names above	52
Lent IV	271	O Bread of life from heaven	53
Lent V	88	O sacred Head, now wounded	54
Palm Sunday	74	All glory, laud, and honor	55
Good Friday	70	O Lamb of God most holy	56
Easter Day	94	That Easter Day with joy was bright	57
Easter I	98	Christ Jesus lay in death's strong bands	58
Easter II	530	The King of love my shepherd is	59
Easter III	100	Alleluia! Jesus lives!	60
Easter IV	167	Holy God, we praise thy Name	61
Easter V	460	O God, eternal source of love	62
Ascension	114	Look, ye saints, the sight is glorious	63
Sunday after Ascension	431	Crown him with many crowns	64
Pentecost	122	Come, Holy Spirit, God and Lord	65
Trinity Sunday	134	Father most holy	66
Trinity I	374	God calling yet	67
Trinity II	151	Built on a rock	69
Trinity III	169	All people that on earth do dwell	70
Trinity IV	348	Turn back, O man	71
Trinity V	188	Lord Jesus Christ, be present now	73
Trinity VI	178	Eternal God, before thy throne we bend	74

SUNDAY	SBH NO.	HYMN	PAGE
Trinity VII	483	Jesus, thou Joy of loving hearts	75
Trinity VIII	171	Our God, to whom we turn	76
Trinity IX	510	Take my life, and let it be consecrated	77
Trinity X	397	Love divine, all loves excelling	78
Trinity XI	575	Jesus, priceless Treasure	79
Trinity XII	181	My God, how wonderful thou art	80
Trinity XIII	130	Holy Spirit, truth divine	81
Trinity XIV	187	Open now thy gates of beauty	82
Trinity XV	172	Immortal, invisible, God only wise	83
Trinity XVI	132	All glory be to God on high	84
Trinity XVII	202	Awake, my soul, and with the sun	85
Trinity XVIII	342	In Christ there is no east or west	86
Trinity XIX	408	Praise to the Lord	87
Trinity XX	262	Deck thyself with joy and gladness	88
Trinity XXI	155	Lord, keep us steadfast in thy word	89
Trinity XXII	437	Ye watchers and ye holy ones	91
Trinity XXIII	520	Guide me, O thou great Jehovah	92
Trinity XXIV	179	Shepherd of tender youth	93
Trinity XXV	600	O Lord of life	94
Trinity XXVI	197	O happy day	95
Last Sunday after Trinity	7	Wake, awake	96
Reformation	150	A mighty fortress is our God	98
All Saints' Day	144	For all the saints	99

Contributors to Part II

Maurice Anderson, Ewald J. Bash, L. David Brown, Gerhard M. Cartford, Jerry Evenrud, Gaylord S. Fagerland, Ralferd C. Freytag, Frederic Hilary, Albert C. Lehman, Warren C. Leist, Linden J. Lundstrom, Daniel A. Moe, Bernt J. Muus, Loui Novak, James Ode, Ella M. Osten, Dorothy Preus, Olga Romstad, Norma Sands, Marie Walck and Katharine J. Weller.

APPENDIX 100

PART I

Introducing . . .

Hymns—How to Sing Them

MANDUS A. EGGE

With few exceptions congregational singing, at least in American Lutheran churches, is at a low ebb. Perhaps we have taken congregational singing too much for granted. The emphasis has been on trained choirs, and the man in the pew has been forgotten. It has been assumed that he can sing any hymn in the hymnal placed before him, and that he will enjoy singing. Nothing could be more false or more fatal to good congregational singing.

The singing of hymns in a Lutheran church, referring particularly to the hymns in the Service, is part of the liturgy. Hymns are part and parcel of the worship offered to the Lord. Through the hymns, God's people speak to him in prayer, praise, and thanksgiving. It is therefore incumbent on God's people that their singing should be the very best possible. True, God has encouraged his people to "make a joyful noise unto the Lord," but his people can never be satisfied with a "joyful noise," for he has given us voices and the ability to sing, and that talent must also be developed and used for his glory.

Of course, hymns can be rehearsed on Sunday morning, during the Service, but a program for learning hymns as a part of the congregation's comprehensive educational program is far better. If the Sunday worship is for the glory of the Lord, it should be the finished product, the congregation's best. If necessary, hymns can be rehearsed during a five- or ten-minute rehearsal preceding the Service, but again, a total program is to be desired.

As a first step in such a program, an inventory of the congregation's repertory should be made. If no record has been kept, someone ought to work through the Sunday bulletins for the past two to five years and write at the top of the page in a hymnal the date on which the hymn was sung. This copy of the hymnal should be used only for this purpose. Next, an evaluation of the findings ought to be made by the worship leaders: pastor, choir director(s), and organist. Perhaps certain hymns ought to be retired from the congregation's repertory—some hymns do wear out if they are used too frequently; others may not be worthy of constant use. Then a list of hymns which ought to be learned by the congregation and become a part of the repertory should be prepared. Consideration should be given to the church year, Sundays and festivals. The final step in this process is to set up a congregational program, including the church school, confirmation classes, auxiliary organizations, and every activity in the congregation in that program. The program ought to be designed for at least the next five years. The purpose of the program will be to learn the hymns on the list.

In making up the list of hymns to be learned, the selections in the *Hymn of the Week Songbook* should be given priority for several reasons. For one thing, it is a selection of good hymns. Too, hymns for the Sundays and festivals of the church year are included. Finally, and this is very valuable in implementing the program, many aids have been provided for teaching these hymns: the *Hymn of the Week Songbook, A Time for Singing* (the recording of all 62 hymns), *We Sing to God,* (vols. I, II, III) which contain the stories behind the hymns, and this book, *Hymns—How to Sing Them.*

All worship leaders should be enlisted when the program is set up: pastor, choir directors, organist, church school leaders, leaders of auxiliary organizations. If one hymn is chosen for each month, that hymn should be learned in the various schools and organizations, and then be used at a Sunday service after it has been learned.

The families of the church should not be forgotten. Using the hymn-of-the-week program, encourage every family to sing the hymn assigned for the week at family devotions. The *Hymn of the Week Songbook* and the recording *A Time for Singing* are designed for use in the homes. This will take some doing, but it will be well worth the effort, for it will not only stimulate better singing in church but will also encourage families to have daily worship.

The campaign for better congregational singing will need constant encouragement and promotion. References to hymns in sermons and talks, through articles in parish papers and Sunday service bulletins, and in announcements at services (this may be a "necessary" announcement in some churches) will help.

Finally, in some churches it may be necessary to start a campaign for a new organ. Too many churches have been satisfied with "peanut whistles." Except for a few very bold individuals, most people are afraid to sing out unless the accompaniment is strong. It is not volume that is needed—any sound can be amplified and become so loud that it is unbearable—but a tone with "body." Only when a church has an adequate organ will the congregation sing out with full voice.

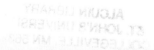

Good and adequate organs are not as expensive today as they were some years ago. Almost any congregation can afford a good instrument. If the church needs a new organ, start an organ fund. It is surprising how quickly such a fund can be gathered if the people of the congregation know about it.

The Apostle Paul wrote, "I will sing with the spirit, and I will sing with understanding also" (I Corinthians 14:15). Let this be the goal in every congregation, and in every family in the church.

Getting Families to Sing at Home

HAROLD J. BELGUM

What picture do you have of the "devotional life" . . . "family altar" . . . "Bible reading" . . . "personal prayers" . . . in the average families of your congregation? Do you believe it could be better? You very likely can't improve it by lecturing or scolding.

You might help by teaching families the hymn-of-the-week, patiently encouraging them to try it, and asking them how it's going. The hymn-of-the-week is Bible-based. In fact, it usually relates to the Gospel for the Sunday. It is devotional. It is a prayer sung. It brings the family together before God in his smallest congregation, the family circle.

Hymn singing is peculiarly suited to family devotional efforts. Why? Well, singing is enjoyed by all ages. Even Grandpa, who can't hear every word when you read, hears the melody and it brings back good memories. Little babies stop fussing when they hear music. Preschoolers pass out the books and collect them.

Pastor: You are holding the key! You are the spiritual leader of the families in your congregation. If you decide that hymn singing would benefit your families, tell them so clearly from the pulpit. Then proceed to plan the Sunday morning worship service so that the hymn-of-the-week is emphasized in some dramatic way. Tell briefly how the hymn is God's Word.

Choir director and organist: Now it's your turn! When the pastor has told how this hymn proclaims the Gospel, you must inspire (that means "breathe into") the congregation the verve, tempo, melody, and rhythm with which you present the hymn. When they have heard one stanza lined out with conviction, invite them to join you. The whole choir may have to sing in unison to fix the melody in their minds, and the organist may have to use a staccato touch to fix the rhythm. If that doesn't do it, bring in trumpets and trombones!

Choir members: It is true that your anthem, well sung, is a special offering to God and a unique gift to the congregation. But consider how brief this experience is on Sunday morning. Think what further blessings you could bring to family suppertimes if your singing of the hymn of the week made them really try it at home. Even by personal conversations with parents and teenagers you may trigger some families into having a go at it.

Church school leaders and teachers: You carry a lot of weight with the children who attend church school. If you use the hymn of the week as your Sunday "theme song," and convey the feeling that singing this at home in the family is the thing to do, it will help tip the balance in many homes. One warning: Be sure you have the hearty cooperation of your pastor. The parents must learn the hymns in church and catch the spirit of the idea from the pastor, otherwise there will not be the teamwork needed around the supper table.

Does it work? In one congregation the pastor was skeptical that anything could get families to sing at home. But he did decide to try an experiment. The Sunday before Advent every member (yes, parents and children) was supplied with a *Hymn of the Week Songbook*. He proposed that every family should sing the hymn of the week after supper during Advent. Each Sunday the pastor commented on the processional hymn. (It was the hymn of the week.) The choir faced the congregation and sang the first stanza in unison. Then the congregation sang the whole hymn. At the end of Advent the pastor asked for a show of hands to indicate how many had been singing at home. More than one-third responded.

The sing-along method: Only one person in a hundred is a monotone. The reason most people do not dare to sing out is that they are uncertain of the melody and rhythm even when they have the words in front of them. The three-record album *A Time for Singing* presents each of the sixty-two hymns-of-the-week sung by a professional group. Here is a whole year of family singing lined out in a most delightful and easy-to-follow way. Make this album known to your families.

The singing family meets God: When we sing hymns we are singing about some part of God's work for our salvation, or about some part of our response to his love for us. The hymn-of-the-week tunes us in to God's concern for us as told clearly in the Gospels for the Christian year.

Teaching Hymns to Pre-Reading Children

BETTY ANN RAMSETH

Music for the little child is an expression of joy. And so the first requisite in teaching hymns to pre-reading children is that you *enjoy* singing with children. A real love for the music of the church is "caught" by them, rather than learned consciously.

Singing a hymn is teaching: so sing, sing, sing! It is not necessary that you be an experienced soloist; it is enough that you sing with enthusiasm, in tune, with clear diction, and with a light, childlike voice that the children will imitate. Sit at the level of the children so they can see your eyes. This is your greatest asset in capturing their interest and holding their attention. You will have greater freedom in teaching if you overlearn your hymns—sing without a hymnal.

First, give a brief, sparkling introduction to the hymn, whether about the composer, the occasion for which it was written, or through a visual aid. Then sing the hymn stanza, without piano accompaniment, so the entire concentration is on the words and the tune. The children need to learn from the beginning to listen and look.

When singing the hymn for the first time, several factors should be observed. (1) Use correct *phrasing*. This teaches the right interpretation from the beginning. (2) Use correct *pitch*. Children naturally have light and airy voices. (3) Have a sense of *rhythm*. Correct tempo gives the spirit of the hymn.

In teaching by rote, which is simply by imitation, either the "whole song" or the "phrase" method is used. In the "whole song" method the entire stanza is imitated by the children. This method may be used for the short, simple hymn. Some hymns may need to be sung many times and over a period of time before the children will be able to sing them. Longer hymns may be made simpler for the preschool child by using just a portion. I call these "hymn sentences" or "hymnlets." Children will grow into them later. (Examples: SBH 443—first line; SBH 433—refrain.)

In using the "phrase" method, first sing the stanza. Then, pointing to yourself, sing the first phrase; next, directing the children, have them imitate it. This is continued through the stanza, without interruption, the rhythm between you and the children never being broken. If they stumble, simply repeat, not stopping to say, "That was wrong." Never talk to correct; just *do* it! Repeat the stanza, phrase by phrase; then, if they seem ready, combine phrases in the same way. Children like to be echoes and sing back to you. A good rule to remember: when you sing, the children listen; when the children sing, you listen.

Children have vivid imaginations, and pointing up a key word or phrase may be all that is necessary to give them an understanding of the hymn. Difficult words should be no obstacle. Some may need synonyms, but the texts will grow in meaning.

Repetition is a basic principle in teaching, but it must be varied and imaginative. (1) Sing *antiphonally:* side against side. (2) *Hum* the melody, teaching the children to make a legato tone similar to that of the organ. (3) *Clap* it! This is a "change of pace" and can also correct a rhythmic problem. (4) *Say* the words, stopping at a key word for them to fill in. (5) Learn a song *backward* by using the refrain first and keeping the stanza for the next session. (Examples: SBH 555, 74, 195) (6) Add piano *accompaniment* after the hymn has been learned. The autoharp is an effective accompanying instrument for some hymns and is appealing to children. (7) Improvise *hand motions* with a few hymns, making unnecessary the use of many of the little ditties used to accomplish the same. (Examples: SBH 443—"with heart, and hands, and voices"; SBH 572—"nestling bird nor star in heaven"; SBH 36—stanza 4—"yet what can I give him —give my heart.") (8) Make a colored *hymn poster* with large letters and pictures. (9) *Sing along* with the *A Time for Singing* recording.

Do not be too concerned when small children do not sing with the class; these very ones may be singing at home. We cannot always know how much they are absorbing, and some do not learn to find their singing voices as soon as others. Be patient! Remember that all children can learn to sing, and they learn to sing by much singing. Encourage them to sing and also to listen at home to the fine recordings available, for if these hymns we are teaching are never used in the home, their value for life may be reduced to a minimum or lost altogether.

Encourage joyous singing, not louder, or the response may become harsh. Ask the children to make their voices "big and round." And lest you forget, thank the children for good singing! It takes such a little praise to get the greatest response from them.

Source materials:
A Time for Singing recording.

Teaching Hymns to Primary Children

MARTI WILSON

We need not deny our children the treasury of great Christian hymns because we feel they may be too young to appreciate them. Appreciation, understanding, association, and enthusiasm for our great hymns are built during the formative years. Primary age children are especially suited to exposure, because their imagination and enthusiasm run high.

When preparing to teach hymns to primary age children, I think in terms of preparing a program for a play. One must consider the author, the setting of the scene, the cast, and the plot.

Author

The children will be able to identify with a composer if they learn some interesting facts about his life and thought. In addition ask your students to contribute. Children love to be involved in the teaching procedure. They will delight in helping to gather material on the composer.

During our hymn study of "Silent Night" we discussed the life of Franz Gruber. This led to a spontaneous playlette using a guitar to illustrate how the accompaniment sounded on that first night when it was sung. We also learned the first stanza of the hymn in German, which made it even more realistic. How much greater is our appreciation of the hymn if we have considered the circumstances under which it was written. Through research we will find something "special" about virtually every great hymn that has been written.

Setting

The setting may be *geographical,* in which case you might show pictures or movies of Bethlehem. The hymn may suggest a *liturgical* setting involving church symbols. We studied the stained glass windows in our church. The children learned how they were made and the meaning of the liturgical symbols. A fitting symbol for the settings of the hymns of Lent was a crown of thorns from the Holy Land. If an *historical* setting is suggested, it will be useful to assist the children to understand the moment in history and to involve them in the precise moment. The imagination of the children will do the rest.

Cast

The cast of the hymn may involve *biblical characters*. It may involve the *church building*, in which case a study of church architecture and symbolism may be made. It may involve *missionaries,* which would suggest a study of a particular mission field. Of course, the most important member of the cast is *God himself*. Religious paintings may be used in picturing the cast, for example:

"O Sacred Head"—"Christ on the Cross," Rubens

"All Glory, Laud and Honor"—"The Triumphal Entry," Plockhorst

"Let All Mortal Flesh Keep Silence"--"The Arrival of the Shepherds," Leroll

Plot

This is most important of all. Does the hymn concern prayer, praise, thanksgiving, service, the church year? Determine the thought the author wishes to convey. As the children learn the words of the hymn let them tell what the words mean to them. They must sing thoughts, not merely sounds. Encourage the children to "think pictures" as they sing. Have them close their eyes when you read the words for the first time.

Having set the mood of the hymn with attention to composer, setting, cast, and plot, the music can carry itself from this point on. Having established the mood and purpose of the hymn, it will "sing itself" and the dynamics will follow quite naturally. The children could accompany the hymn singing using piano, recorder, or autoharp.

With some of these thoughts in mind, consider a series of hymns for long-range study. A hymn notebook for each child is a useful teaching tool. Prepare individual hymn study sheets for inclusion in the notebook outlined as a history of church music based on hymns of each period. This is a good opportunity to examine the plainsong, a hymn form too often overlooked, and also to expose the children to Bach chorales, which are the best examples of our Lutheran musical heritage. The history of hymns reflects the history of the church from earliest times.

The main ingredient underlying any of these presentations is, of course, enthusiasm. Enthusiasm is contagious, and without it the presentation will fail. However, if you ever feel that your sources have run dry, ask the children—they'll never disappoint you!

Source materials:

Bailey, A. E., *The Gospel in Hymns*, Scribners.

Maus, C. P., *Christ and the Fine Arts*, Harper.

Maus, C. P., *The Church and the Fine Arts*, Harper.

Teaching Hymns to Juniors

RONALD A. NELSON

"Today, boys and girls," announces the junior worship leader, "we are going to learn a new hymn. Turn to number six on your song sheets. Now this is a joyful song of praise, so we must really sing out! Mrs. Johnson, would you give us the starting chord, please? Now, let's really hear it!"

The pianist plays the hymn, to the accompaniment of a faint murmur of voices vainly trying to pick the melody from the full chords. The worship leader does not sing. Instead she cups her hands to her ear, and, when the murmuring is finally over, exclaims, "Boys and girls! I couldn't even *hear* you! This is a song of *praise!* Now let's do it again, and *really sing!*"

Hopelessly the routine is repeated exactly as before. Then comes the crowning blow. With a gleam in her eye the leader says, "Why, some of you aren't singing at all. I want to hear *only the boys* sing the second stanza."

To the accompaniment of the giggling girls surrounding them, the boys, slouching as low as possible in their seats, knowing that defeat is certain, somehow manage to agonize through the second stanza, awaiting the tongue-lashing which is sure to follow.

Several titles might be given to the above story—"How to Discourage Hymn-singing Without Really Trying," "How to Prevent Children from Learning a Hymn," or even "How to Perpetuate the Theory that Boys Can't Sing." The real tragedy, of course, is that this story actually happens every week in many parishes throughout the country. Let us use it as a stimulus toward finding a better way.

Obviously these juniors had no real opportunity to learn the hymn. True, they had the words before them, but none had ever heard the melody. The tune was not provided for them in written form, and neither were they exposed to it in any other way.

In an average group of juniors there will probably be few who can read notes well enough to sing them at sight. But why insult the abilities of these few by limiting our teaching to rote method? Both words and tune should be provided in written form. At least the first stanza and the tune could be written on the blackboard.

Modern music education is rediscovering the value of listening. The greater the opportunity for repeated listening before singing, the fewer the mistakes when we sing. This applies to any age-group. One of the tasks of the hymn teacher, then, is to create varied and interesting opportunities for *hearing* the hymn. A few possibilities might be:

1. Good recordings.

2. Piano. Use the hymns for prelude and postlude (while children are coming and going) for several weeks before they are to be learned.

3. A soloist could be the leader, or better yet a gifted child who has learned the hymn ahead of time.

4. The junior choir, which has pre-learned the hymn in its own separate rehearsal periods.

5. Another instrument, played by a gifted child from the group, well prepared ahead of time. The tune may be played with or without piano accompaniment, both before and during the learning process.

What about the background of the hymns? Should juniors know something about author and composer?

The answer depends on how interesting and stimulating such information will be. Will it be worth the time it will take? Will it capture the imagination of this hero-worshiping age group?

More important than background is the meaning of the hymn. What is it trying to say? Do the youngsters understand all of the words? (Sometimes a sudden stop in the middle of a stanza with the question, "What does that mean?" will liven up the session.) Is there biblical or doctrinal background which should be discussed? Do they realize, in singing "Lord, keep us steadfast in thy word," that each stanza is addressed to one person of the Trinity? In approaching the meaning of the hymn it is always best to let *them* tell *you* rather than you giving a lecture. Volunteers may be assigned some dictionary or Bible "homework" to be completed by the next session and shared with the group.

What about the voice quality of juniors? Is there time for work on this? Probably not, but this doesn't mean we must be satisfied with ugly sounds. Sometimes the simple admonition, "Make it beautiful!" will transform a familiar hymn from a yell to lively but lovely music.

Once the mechanics of teaching are absorbed, the most important advice to a hymn teacher would probably be, "Forget your dignity! Make it fun!"

Source materials:

A Time for Singing recording.
Great Hymns for Children recording.
Great Lutheran Hymns recording.

Teaching Hymns to Confirmands and Adults

THOMAS E. HERBRANSON

Three key considerations will help leaders make hymn singing enjoyable and valuable for singers from 13 to 113 years of age.

1. The theology of the words is of prime importance. Martin Luther used music's beauty and popularity to carry the scriptural message to the people. Today, most people tend to concentrate on the tune (music) rather than the hymn (poetic words). Leaders must attempt to change this. Confirmands and adults should be trained to look more critically at the words, asking, "Is what we are singing really biblical?" "Maybe we shouldn't sing stanza three?" "Could we honestly sing it?"

It may well be very difficult for a leader to discover sound scriptural interpretation. Nevertheless, maturing Christians have a responsibility to dig into the total message of a hymn with no less inquiry than into a scriptural text. In asking questions about the content of a hymn, look for what the author says in the following biblical categories:

God, Man, Christ, Spirit, Church, Sacraments, Last Things, Christian Life. What different names and actions express each one? Which are emphasized? Which are missing?

It is not enough to recall the background of the hymn, the season of the church year, and the character of the hymn. Study the words. What is behind the word pictures and unfamiliar words? Confirmation material of The American Lutheran Church directs youth toward a systematic method in studying the Bible, a procedure that could well be used for studying hymns:

    a. Pray the Holy Spirit to communicate the meaning of the words.

    b. Ask yourself, "What does this hymn mean to me?"

    c. Define words and word pictures. Use a Bible dictionary.

    d. Ask questions to discover main content: Who? What? Where? When? How? Why?

    e. Look for comparisons and contrasts, causes and effects, means to ends, and repetitions, not only in one stanza but between stanzas (i.e. *never* sing just the first stanza of "A Mighty Fortress," for the Evil One is victor at this point; or see relationships of Father, Son, Holy Spirit between stanzas).

2. Rhyme and repetition are "hooks" for memorizing. There is great satisfaction in having a repertoire of hymns that congregational groups can sing "at the drop of a hat, in the park or in the dark." Few hymnals are regularly used in the home. Only the wider Christian family of leagues, circles, board meetings, studies, retreats, and of course congregational worship, gives opportunities for fixing great hymns in our memories. Those times come when no hymnals are available, so, because we dare not chance stumbling through a fine hymn, we don't sing at all. What riches the person has who can recall the great hymns of the faith in times of joy, sorrow, change and growth, birth and death!

Memorizing always requires a measure of struggle, no matter what method is used. Yet it can be fun and challenging to master the message and the music. Here is one method:

a. Highlight the message, stanza development, and theological interpretation.

b. On chalkboard, pictorialize the content of each stanza. Let the group suggest what they see.

c. Note rhyming words in each stanza and the difference between true and false rhyme (e.g. Lord, blood). Both serve as memory aids. Repeat rhymed words with the group.

d. Master a stanza by singing it after each of the first three steps. Remember, repetition is the mother of learning. Now sing it without books.

e. Competition can make memorizing fun. Have men memorize one stanza, women another, soloist or leader another. Don't give up!

Here is a list of hymns-of-the-week that could be memorized and used for many occasions: SBH 21, 271, 188, 181, 408, 150.

3. Rhythm is the accent of our generation. Young and old alike appreciate the pulse and beat we call rhythm, whether it be in a sophisticated symphony or in a syncopated folk song. Calling all hymn leaders and organists: give the notes their proper value, and watch the phrasing so that the rhythm of the words and music can bring out all the hymn is trying to say.

Concern for rhythm does not mean abandoning the church hymn for gospel songs with piano or twanging guitar. But perhaps we should look with more care for the hymns we do have that hold a good message and music *and* an interesting rhythmic pattern. How about these? SBH 19, 94, 144, 351, 530.

Do you want your congregation to sing with more understanding, confidence, and appreciation? If so, your leadership must convey the importance of the word's message, the value of memorizing, and the enjoyment of rhythm.

Congregational Hymn Rehearsals

KATHRYN ULVILDEN MOEN

Martin Luther believed the Christian church should be a singing church. He took parts of the liturgy formerly assigned to the clergy or choir and gave them to the congregation to sing. He revised Latin hymns, provided new texts for old songs, wrote melodies of his own, and encouraged others to do the same. He urged music instruction in the schools, made a place for choirs in his services, commended hymn singing at family devotions, and wrote fan letters to his favorite composer. Moreover, at Wittenberg the entire congregation regularly met during the week to rehearse the hymns and responses for the coming Sunday.[1]

Four and a half centuries later we dismiss these rehearsals as a quaint aspect of an innovating, reforming, and unhurried age. We dismiss them, that is, until a musicologist like Joseph N. Ashton reminds us to look at our present circumstances:

> The congregation is the only musical group of serious purpose regularly attempting performance without rehearsing. The choir, composed though it is of the more musically capable ones, finds it necessary to meet for practice, but the comparatively unmusical congregation scarcely ever makes a pretense at such a thing. . . . It seems tacitly and all too readily assumed that the congregation can sing at sight anything to be found between the two covers of the hymnbook. The ineffectiveness of congregational music shows the falsity of this assumption.[2]

Another observer, Søren Kierkegaard, jolts complacency again when he reminds us that at a church service, the congregation is not an audience assembled to hear and see a program. Rather, God is the audience, and the congregation the actors. Sporadic, indifferent, slovenly hymn singing constitutes a poor performance.[3] The company needs rehearsing.

Two important difficulties, of course, are that the matter is not generally regarded as one of primary importance, and the calendar is crowded. The pastor might prepare the way for a change in attitude in sermons about the true meaning of corporate worship and the rich rewards to be gained from even a rudimentary knowledge of hymnody. Notes in service bulletins or the parish paper about the authors, composers, and liturgical relevance of hymns to be sung at coming services may call attention to the broad topic. A brief song service at a congregational dinner or other gathering might prepare the way for a rehearsal by showing that group hymn singing can be very enjoyable. In any case, the rehearsal should not be announced without a concerted, carefully worked-out effort to tell the people what is intended, and to persuade them that they will enjoy and profit from attending.

A Sunday morning service is for worship, not practice, and congregational hymn rehearsals ideally should not be scheduled at that hour. A special Sunday evening or weekday hour would be preferable—a Reformation custom which persists in present-day Germany and other parts of Europe. Perhaps a rehearsal could be held in conjunction with some other event, such as a congregational meeting or special service. But if circumstances prevent people from participating in appreciable numbers at other times, then the hymn rehearsal could be held at the time of the Sunday service— perhaps in lieu of the opening liturgy or even as a substitute for the sermon. Thus, on rehearsal Sunday, the Word would be conveyed in song.

Hymns to be learned at the rehearsals should be selected according to an over-all, long-range plan. Perhaps no congregation can claim familiarity or even exposure to *all* the 602 hymns in the *Service Book and Hymnal*. Each one has what might be termed its own repertoire. The pastor, church music staff, representatives of the deacons, and the music committee might study the Sunday bulletin file and survey the hymnal in an effort to identify this repertoire. The next step is to determine what important but missing hymns should be added, and what familiar but inferior ones should be slowly allowed to fade into disuse. Three articles by Carl F. Pfatteicher in the *Journal of Church Music* help to identify what these additions and deletions might be.[4]

In general, the hymn rehearsal should not be long and the time should not be over-occupied by classroom talk. It should begin and end with something familiar, and it should be conducted vigorously by a choir director or layman with a good singing voice, a gift for informal leadership, and enthusiasm for the task at hand. Members of the choir might be scattered through the congregation to reinforce the singing. Text as well as music should be considered, for a few comments about the source, history, or application of the words of a hymn help the people sing it with understanding and conviction.

The leader should identify the new hymns carefully before the rehearsal, identifying repeated notes, phrases, or lines; making note of possible pitfalls; and deciding upon the best strategy for effective teaching and efficient learning. At the rehearsal, the texts should be read aloud and then the melody played through. The leader may begin to teach by rote, singing the hymn himself, according to his strategy, with the congregation repeating after him—all singing the melody in unison and without accompaniment. From the very beginning, he must be especially careful to establish, communicate, and maintain a steady rhythm appropriate to the hymn being studied. As soon as initial difficulties have been surmounted, the congregation can practice the hymn by singing the second and remaining stanzas.

Using a variety of procedures might be a way of maintaining interest. The more familiar hymns may be sung antiphonally, or, where possible, in canon form. The organist may use an alternate harmonization, and the choir members might sing an occasional descant or four-part harmony. A hymn quiz or a brief explanation of musical terms and symbols could be the means of providing a constructive break in the singing. The rehearsal can end on a positive note by inviting everyone present to join in a familiar hymn of service or dedication.

Care should be taken to repeat as soon as possible and more than once all of the freshly learned hymns presented at the rehearsal in the form of anthems or organ works as well as congregational hymns. The service bulletin should call attention to these uses of the melodies.

Four words summarize this discussion: motivation, preparation, careful presentation, and repetition. Congregational hymn rehearsals conducted with these in mind can be an effective approach to the problem of improving congregational song.

FOOTNOTES

[1] Roland Bainton, *Here I Stand* (Nashville: Abingdon 1950), 346.

[2] Joseph N. Ashton, *Music in Worship* (Boston: Pilgrim Press 1943), 94.

[3] Austin C. Lovelace & William C. Rice, *Music and Worship in the Church* (Nashville: Abingdon 1960), 147.

[4] Carl F. Pfatteicher, "Better Hymn Tunes and Better Congregational Singing," *Journal of Church Music* 7:11:4-6; Part 2, "Chorales," *Ibid.*, 8:1:12-14; Part 3, "Psalmody," *Ibid.*, 8:2:10-12.

Use of Instruments with Hymn Singing

VERNON C. KNUTSON

A valuable source for embellishing hymn singing lies relatively untapped in many communities—the public school instrumental music department. A wealth of talent has been developed in this area; we should use its products more extensively. What better way to add dimension to our church music than to use these instruments and this talent to glorify God!

A canvass of your parish will disclose the number and types of instrumentalists. A variety of ensembles might be formed, such as:

1. Trios and quartets of like instruments (cornet, clarinet, flute, trombone, saxophone).

2. Smaller mixed ensembles (cornets and trombones, flutes and clarinets, clarinets and trumpets).

3. Larger ensembles which use a combination of instruments.

4. Ensembles of stringed orchestral instruments (violin, viola, 'cello, etc.).

When and where ought an instrumental ensemble to be used? A variety of possibilities exist:

The Service

Perhaps a new hymn can be introduced by the ensemble with organ or piano. Or, could you schedule a congregational hymn rehearsal ten minutes before the service, or in place of the organ prelude? A wind ensemble used at this point would be ready to aid with the opening hymn as well. For instance, a trio of trumpets or a brass quartet of trumpets and trombones could be used for a hymn such as "Praise to the Lord" (SBH 408).

Fanfares, Chorale Preludes, Intradas

Opportunities for pageantry, performed in good taste, appear in these music types and will help to establish an added zest on a festival day.

Youth Programs

Luther League meetings and the vacation church school afford excellent platforms for young instrumentalists. Hymn arrangements, either as accompaniment or program material, can be used to advantage in these settings. The technical facility displayed by the younger players will usually be better accepted in these types of meetings. A training ground is thus provided for more mature work at a later age.

Hymn Festivals

Exciting possibilities abound in the hymn festival area. Hymn accompaniment, modulation material, and antiphonal work serve as excellent vehicles for bringing instrumental music into its own as an important contributor to a varied hymn festival.

Though there is not a great deal of ensemble literature available for hymn singing accompaniment, it can easily and readily be transposed. The lack of knowledge of transposition should not be a serious problem, for even if the players themselves cannot transpose while playing, they can learn to write the transpositions. The following brief guide may be of help:

Bb Instruments: (cornet, soprano clarinet, bass clarinet, tenor saxophone, etc.). Transpose by raising the piano score notes by one degree (from a space to the next line, or from a line to the next space) and altering the key signature by subtracting two flats or adding two sharps. Example:

Eb Instruments: (alto saxophone, alto horn, alto clarinet). Transpose by raising the piano score notes by six degrees or lowering by three degrees and altering the key signature by subtracting three flats or adding three sharps, or combination thereof. Example:

F Instruments: (French horn in F, English horn). Transpose by raising the piano score notes by five degrees or lowering four degrees and altering the key signature by subtracting one flat or adding one sharp. Example:

In forming workable ensemble combinations, one must keep in mind the characteristics and ranges of the instruments involved. The clarinets, flutes, and cornets are primarily soprano and alto instruments and should generally be playing those voice parts. The trombones, baritones, and larger saxophones are best used for the tenor and bass voice parts.

A recent noteworthy development has appeared in some churches, that of the appointment of a Director of Instrumental Music. This is to be encouraged, even though coupled with another position such as choir director or organist. This person could be given the latitude necessary to plan for instrumentalists on festival days, to assist performers with their transpositions as well as with their playing, and generally to work closely with the pastor and the music committee for the best use of ensembles.

Hymn Festivals

KATHRYN ULVILDEN MOEN

A thoughtfully planned hymn festival, involving one or more congregations, choirs, and instrumentalists can be an instructive, inspiring, and gloriously beautiful occasion. It offers an excellent means of persuading people to sing old favorites with new attention, and to try less familiar melodies or forms of accompaniment without fear of being taken unaware.

Although the hymn festival has no liturgy or set form, it is a service, not just a church celebration or community sing. It begins and ends with devotions, and it is organized around a selected theme, topic, festival, or message.

The indexes at the back of the *Service Book and Hymnal* suggest a variety of themes, for they include lists of authors, translators, composers, tune names, sources, topics, and first lines. A festival could be based upon the life of Christ in song; the liturgical year in hymns; the Creed in hymns; hymns by famous authors or composers; chorales in the hymnal; songs the reformers sang; women hymn writers; hymns based upon the 23rd Psalm; kinds of hymns (psalms, plainsong, Latin hymns, chorales, spirituals, American folk songs, contemporary hymns); hymns from various centuries; hymns for the coming season; the house of God; hymns of faith, confession, etc.

The hymns relating to the theme are arranged into groups separated by appropriate readings from Scripture, the Psalms, or prayers. The message given by the pastor might relate to the theme, or discuss the lives and beliefs of the men whose work is being presented.

But the hymns comprise the major portion of the service. They should be presented in a great variety of ways: antiphonally, with one side of the church singing one line, the other the next; contrasting voices, women one stanza or phrase, men another, children a third—perhaps with their elders humming; a cappella, either in unison or four-part harmony (unaccompanied unison singing can be very impressive).

Choirs can play an important part in a hymn festival. If several congregations are cooperating, separate choirs can be placed in various parts of the church; transepts, gallery, front, rear, echoing each other, or repeating a final line or phrase. Unison congregational singing of one stanza can be followed by the choir singing a stanza in parts or an anthem based on a hymn. Small groups from the choir can introduce unfamiliar melodies. Descants can bring some hymns to a thrilling conclusion.

The organist can also help the congregation with less familiar hymns by playing the melody alone or an octave above the other parts or on a solo stop such as a reed, with the other three parts on another manual. Alternate harmonizations may be used in a portion of a familiar hymn, provided the congregation understands what is being done. A chorale prelude or other hymn-related composition can be used to introduce a hymn, or as an organ interlude between hymn groups. Using an intrada, a concertato, or another special hymn arrangement for congregation, choir, instruments, and organ can provide a fine climax for the entire service.

The purpose of all this variety is to focus attention upon the *meaning* of the hymns. Each form of presentation should be devised with an eye upon the message to be communicated. Occasionally the congregation should be invited to read a stanza silently while the organist plays it. Sometimes a stanza should be read aloud without any music at all.

With careful planning, willing choirs, and a good organist, the people attending a hymn festival will learn things about hymns, the hymnal, organ literature, and festive accompaniments which will sharpen perceptions, deepen understanding, and arouse enthusiasm. Almost in spite of themselves, they will sing with attention and spirit never before experienced. Once tried, the festival probably will become an annual event. And it will have served its purpose if wholehearted and intelligent hymn singing becomes a custom in the Lutheran home and a characteristic of the Lutheran church service—everywhere!

Source materials:

Reginald L. McAll, *The Hymn Festival Movement in America.* Paper number XVI, Hymn Society of America, 1951.

HYMN FESTIVAL
Based on the Nicene Creed

PRELUDE

INVOCATION

THE NICENE CREED—First Article (Congregation)

Narrator: Malachi 2:10; Ephesians 2:10; Psalm 104:24

Hymn 163—O WORSHIP THE KING

Stanza 1: Children's choir	Stanza 4: Congregation
Stanza 2: Congregation	Stanza 5: All choirs
Stanza 3: Choir	Stanza 6: Congregation

Narrator: Psalm 103:19-22

Hymn 172—IMMORTAL, INVISIBLE

1: Congregation	3: Women
2: Choir	4: Congregation

THE NICENE CREED—Second Article (Congregation)

Narrator: John 1:1-5

Hymn 17—OF THE FATHER'S LOVE BEGOTTEN

1: Children's choir	3: Choir men
2: Women	4: Congregation
	5: Congregation

Narrator: John 1:9-12

Hymn 42—GOD OF GOD, LIGHT OF LIGHT (Stanzas 2 and 3)

2: Congregation	3: Congregation

Narrator: Philippians 2:5-11

Hymn 501—O JESU SO MEEK

1: Choir	2: Congregation

Narrator: Luke 2:10b-12

Hymn 21—ALL PRAISE TO THEE

1: Congregation	4: Congregation, in canon: Pulpit
2: Choir, in canon	side begins, lectern side enters
3: Children's choir, in canon	four notes later.

5: Congregation, in unison

Narrator: Isaiah 53:5-6

Hymn 88—O SACRED HEAD, NOW WOUNDED

1: Congregation	3: Congregation
2: Organ	4: Organ

Narrator: Matthew 28:5b-7

Hymn 109—GOOD CHRISTIAN MEN, REJOICE AND SING!

1: Men	3: Congregation
2: Women	4: Congregation

Narrator: Acts 1:8-9
Hymn 114—LOOK, YE SAINTS (second tune)

1: Choir	3: Organ
2: Congregation	4: Congregation

Narrator: Acts 1:10-11
Hymn 343—JUDGE ETERNAL

1: Choir	3: Congregation
2: Congregation, a cappella	

Narrator: Matthew 10:32-40, 42
Hymn 351—WHERE CROSS THE CROWDED WAYS OF LIFE

1: Congregation	4: Congregation
2: Organ	5: Men
3: Children's choir	6: Congregation

THE NICENE CREED—Third Article (Congregation)
Narrator: Acts 2:1-4
Hymn 126—COME, O COME, THOU QUICKENING SPIRIT

1: Children's choir	3: Choir
2: Congregation	4: Congregation

Narrator: Acts 2:29-33, 36
Hymn 149—THE CHURCH'S ONE FOUNDATION

1: Congregation	3: Organ
2: Congregation	4: Congregation

Narrator: Acts 2:38-39
Hymn 259—HE THAT BELIEVES AND IS BAPTIZED

1: Congregation	2: Congregation

Narrator: I John 3:1-2
Hymn 572—CHILDREN OF THE HEAVENLY FATHER

1: All children	3: Congregation
2: Men	4: Congregation, in harmony, without organ

Narrator: Revelation 7:9, 10, 13-17
Hymn 144—FOR ALL THE SAINTS (first tune)

1: Congregation	5: Organ
2: Congregation	6: Congregation
3: Congregation	7: Organ
4: Choir	8: Congregation

BENEDICTION

POSTLUDE

PART II

ADVENT I
Songbook—1
SBH—11

O How Shall I Receive Thee

Motivation

The joyous, bright character of the tune is appealing to children as well as adults. The tune is also set to the text "All glory, laud, and honor," and this can be used to show the similarity between Advent and Palm Sunday. The expectation implied should be emphasized.

The author of this hymn is Paul Gerhardt, one of the most famous of Lutheran hymn writers. He lived in the 17th century and wrote this hymn during the time of the Thirty Years' War.

Presentation

Most of the tune lies in a medium range suitable for children as well as adults. However, the first and last notes (middle C) need to be approached carefully. The first note should not be accented but rather thought of as a springboard to the next note. This will keep the voice light and help to steer away from a heavy chest tone, especially in the children's voices.

Time should be spent on the text for children. The imagery and the words are often beyond their comprehension. A few words of explanation can make the text meaningful to them. It would be well to read the Gospel for the First Sunday in Advent, Matthew 21:1-9, on which this hymn is based. Then discuss the account of Jesus' entry into Jerusalem, relating it to the season of Advent when we look forward to the commemoration of his coming as the Christ Child as well as to his second coming.

Application

A flute could be used to play the melody with the singing of the hymn, or the flute alone could be used to play the introduction of the tune before the congregation sings it. With the text "All glory, laud, and honor" the arrangements by Richard Purvis* and Miles Johnson* for brass ensemble are very effective with congregational singing.

Organ chorale preludes on this tune are available in the following collections: *Hymntune Preludes,* Vol. I*; *Liturgical Chorale Book*;* and *Seasonal Chorale Preludes for Manuals Only,* Book 1*.

---

*See appendix.

| # Lift Up Your Heads, Ye Mighty Gates

"Stir up, we beseech thee, thy power, O Lord, and come . . . . "
"Stir up our hearts, O Lord, to make ready the way of thine only
begotten Son . . . . " In this manner the collects for the first and second Sundays in Advent begin. Such evocative prayer language calls
for a matching strength of poetic and musical utterance in the hymns
for this season of the Church Year. "Lift up your heads, ye mighty
gates" possesses these qualities, and its use during Advent will
greatly enrich both private and corporate devotional life.

The text of the hymn sounds a note of triumph at the entry of
the King of glory. It is based on Psalm 24, especially verse 7, which
reads: "Lift up your heads, O gates, and be lifted up, O ancient
doors, that the King of glory may come in." It would be well, however, to consider the entire Psalm as background. The hymn was
written for use on the First Sunday in Advent by Georg Weissel
(1590-1635), a German Lutheran pastor, who was one of the important hymn writers of this period. Catherine Winkworth (1829-
1878), noted for her outstanding translations of German hymns into
English, is responsible for this translation.

The study of this hymn should also take into account the second
version as it appears in the *Service Book and Hymnal*. The first version is, in fact, an abbreviation of the second and simply utilizes
the first four lines of stanzas 1, 3, and 4. The composer of the tune,
Truro (the name of a town in Cornwall, England), is unknown. It
first appeared in a collection of Thomas Williams in 1789. An interesting keyboard introduction to this hymn might well be the first
phrase of "Joy to the world," which happens to be an almost exact
inversion (play it backwards) of the first phrase of *Truro*. This
writer has found the hymn to be a great favorite of his children
whose Advent celebration is marked by enthusiastic and repeated
renditions.

Comfort, Comfort Ye, My People

"Comfort, comfort ye, my people" is an adaptation of Isaiah 40:1-8. Although it was originally written for the festival of St. John the Baptist and based on the Epistle for that day, it is particularly appropriate for our worship during the Advent season. The writer of this hymn was Johann Olearius, who compiled a 17th century hymnbook and also wrote a commentary on the Bible.

The words are contemplative, and the hymnal's suggestion to sing this hymn "brightly" seems initially out of place. But when we take the text in its proper setting as well as in the season of Advent, it becomes clear that the words are anticipatory and are to be sung in a manner showing that we are excited, yes, overjoyed about our Lord's coming.

This hymntune is among those in our hymnal which are habitually incorrectly sung and accompanied. The meter is 6/4-8/4 and the hymn is meant to be counted precisely. The rests are *half rests* and give the over-all hymn true form and character only if they are observed correctly. When the hymn is sung "brightly" the rests become assets to singers' breathing and make this hymn comfortable as well as exciting. The singing must be done with spirit and vitality (enthusiasm).

It is interesting to note that a similar melody with quite different rhythm is found for hymns 71 and 194 *(Service Book and Hymnal)*. The latter two are adaptations and harmonizations by J. S. Bach. However, all three hymns are called *Psalm 42* or *Freu dich sehr* and come from the *Genevan Psalter, 1551,* either composed or arranged by Louis Bourgeois. But in the *Service Book and Hymnal,* No. 12 remains unique, a mighty Advent hymn, a source of great inspiration and worship for us in our praise of God who alone can comfort his people and give us peace.

O Come, O Come, Emmanuel

"Behold, a virgin shall conceive and bear a son, and his name shall be called Emmanuel (which means, God with us)" (Matthew 1:23).

This hymn of longing and joy for the coming of the Savior is one of the great hymns of Advent. Several facts make it unique.

The Text

The medieval antiphons known as the "Great O Antiphons" are the basis of the text. There are seven of these antiphons or responses, each beginning with the letter "O" and followed by an Old Testament name for the Messiah. In the original order they are: Wisdom, Lord, Root of Jesse, Key of David, Dayspring, King, and Emmanuel. These antiphons were used as a response before and after the psalm for the last seven days in Advent, December 17-23. Later they were set in rhymed stanzas with an added refrain. John Mason Neale translated five of them from the Latin.

The Music

This is a plainsong melody. Unlike most of our hymns, this is not measured music with strong accents. Rather it is in free rhythm flowing with the phrasing of the text. It is a mistake to attempt to put it into a "time" pattern. All voices should sing the melody in unison to create the most authentic sound. Harmony is added to the melody only to satisfy our ears so accustomed to four-part sound.

Singing the Hymn

1. Introduce the hymn with a few remarks about the text and the music.

2. Have the group find the names of the Messiah at the beginning of each stanza.

3. With the group read the first stanza, noting where the strongest syllables fall.

4. Play the melody only. Point out the syllables which get more than one note.

5. Sing the first stanza, the voices rising and falling with the melodic line.

6. Read the refrain, observing the proper punctuation. Sing the refrain with no break between "Emmanuel" and "shall."

7. Repeat the procedure for the other stanzas. Sing alternately with boys and men, girls and women.

36

From Heaven Above to Earth I Come

One of the most beautiful of the German family Christmas customs is to gather around the piano on Christmas Eve to sing carols. The *Gemütlichkeit* of such an occasion cannot be translated into any English expression without distortion or sentimentality. Its meaning is felt to some extent when we think of our own families at Christmas time, with perhaps a few intimate friends, and the warmth of togetherness that the music of Christmas can bring. The love, the anticipation of the gifts to be opened, and thankfulness for the privilege of being together once more—thankfulness especially for the intimacy and tenderness of God's gift of a Child that symbolized the eternal renewal of hope for a world that is tired of sin—all these feelings crowd our hearts.

Martin Luther often planned such a Christmas Eve for his family. In 1534 he planned a special entertainment for his children. A man dressed as an angel visited their festive carol sing and brought a new song. He was to sing the first seven stanzas and they were to respond with eight more. The song was *Ich komm aus fremden Landen her.* They sang it to a folk tune, a typical popular sacred song of the day. The new song was none other than Luther's beloved Christmas hymn, "From heaven above to earth I come," which he later set to a new tune and published in 1539.

It was not unusual in those days to sing carols of such length. The idea of the biblical narrative is understood only in the hymn's entirety. To understand it, first read Luke 2:1-18, then read the 15 stanzas of the hymn. Some hymnals such as *The Lutheran Hymnal* (Concordia Publishing House) and *The Lutheran Hymnary* (Augsburg Publishing House) contain the entire hymn. You might also compare the new, and possibly better, translation by Roland Bainton in *The Story of Our Hymns* by Armin Haeussler (Eden Publishing House), which retains the simpler, childlike language of the original.

In presenting the hymn, sing it according to the setting in the *Service Book and Hymnal.* For variety, if a choir is available, sing one or two stanzas in the Bach setting (SBH 34). It would also be valuable, for greater interest, to have the choir sing a version of this hymn from Bach's *Christmas Oratorio.*

All Praise to Thee, Eternal Lord

Martin Luther, who is credited with writing the present text of this hymn, never ceased to be amazed at the staggering truth that the eternal, almighty Son of God came to us in the form of human flesh. He preached and wrote of this theme often as a mighty demonstration of the Father's love. It is so large a fact as not to be contained unless expressed in what we call a "paradox." To express truth in a paradox simply means that in order to say the whole truth two apparently contradictory things must be stated that go counter to what seems to be common sense. The Christmas story is such a truth. Note the following paradoxes:

The eternal Lord is clothed in flesh and blood.

A manger becomes a throne.

One to whom the heavens bow is unfolded in a mother's arms.

The little child gives the old and weary rest.

His lowly birth gives cause for us to rise to the heavens.

Coming in the darksome night, he makes us children of light.

The music is from the very old tune, written by the "Father of English Church Music," Thomas Tallis. It is familiar as a setting for the famous evening hymn of Thomas Ken (SBH 223). This hymn is a canon which is written so that the tenor part takes the same melody as the soprano only five notes following. For this reason it is often used as a round. Thomas Tallis believed strongly in congregational singing and was influenced by the Reformation to this end. He contributed many hymns with a simple harmony that flow in majesty and power. With the exception of Palestrina, no other Christian musician influenced the 16th century as much.

This hymn is ideal for singing as a round. Dividing into groups, each one would begin four notes later. In the first stanza this would occur after the words "thee," "Lord," "garb," "blood," etc. End the round by singing in unison the last stanza as a statement of dignified joy.

38

Let All Mortal Flesh Keep Silence

Though this hymn is placed among the hymns for Holy Communion in the *Service Book and Hymnal,* because of its reference to "the Body and the Blood," it is an excellent hymn for the Christmas season, particularly for the Second Sunday after Christmas. The melody is one of the few tunes from France in the hymnal, but one of the most intriguing and beautiful tunes in the entire hymnal.

An effective way to introduce this hymn would be to have the adult choir sing one of several available anthems based on the hymn.* This should be followed by a brief modulation leading directly into the hymn. Using the anthem as an introduction will help the congregation to learn the tune as well as to appreciate the beauty of the hymn. For variety in singing, have all the men sing stanzas one and two. The tune is particularly well adapted to male voices because of its style and range. On stanza three, have the women and children join the men, but sing this stanza without accompaniment. On stanza four, add the accompaniment. This hymn should be sung in unison throughout.

Directing this hymn takes a bit of doing. The melody is similar to Gregorian chant, and should therefore be directed with a circular motion, rather than trying to beat quarter notes or half notes. It should be sung as a folktune. Though the notes have value, the rhythm should not be "wooden" or stiff. "In flowing style," is a good way of saying this. (By the way, be sure you know where each syllable of the word "alleluia" falls in the last stanza. The first "alleluia" has five notes, the second six, and the third five. It is sung, al-le-lu-i-a.)

In introducing this hymn, reference might be made to Isaiah's vision, Isaiah 6:1-8. A comparison of the poem with the scriptural text could be very interesting.

---

*See appendix.

EPIPHANY
Songbook—8
SBH—404

How Brightly Beams the Morning Star

Motivation

Have you ever noticed a morning star? It shines bright and clear in the eastern sky even after the other stars have faded from sight. This hymn is something like a bright star. It expresses joy and confidence. No one would ever think that it was written during a time of great sorrow.

Pastor Philipp Nicolai wrote the words of this hymn at the time of a dreadful epidemic. In the village where he was pastor, 1,300 people died during a period of six months. One day alone thirty graves had to be dug. Day by day the pastor studied his Bible to find words of hope and comfort for his people. It was then he wrote this hymn.

Pastor Nicolai also composed the tune for his hymn. The hymn became very popular not only in Germany but in Norway and Denmark. It was frequently used for weddings. It is said that many church chimes were set to this stirring melody. You will find this tune used for several other hymns in our hymnal.

This hymn is often called the "Queen of Chorales." Pastor Nicolai wrote the words and composed the tune of another hymn which became known as the "King of Chorales." It is the glorious hymn "Wake, awake, for night is flying."

Presentation

Print or write the words of the first stanza on a large chart so all can see the words clearly.

Tell some interesting facts about the hymn.

Read the stanza together. Underline and discuss such words as: *doth, pining, bestowing.*

Explain that the poet is not writing about a real star. He is thinking of Jesus. Read John 8:12 and Revelation 22:16.

Use a picture or the symbol of the church season for which the hymn is to be used. Encourage children to cut stars in various shapes from colored paper or foil to be placed on the chart.

Ask the pianist to play the *melody notes only* as you point to the words on the chart. Vary this by using the record *A Time for Singing.* After listening to the hymn, suggest that the group sing along.

Of the Father's Love Begotten

Read the text of the hymn before singing it. What are the themes of the hymn? Other than the sounds of another age in the words, what unusual notes does the text strike? What scripture passages come to mind when you read? An Ohio church once had a controversy within the congregation over a new art glass window. The nativity scene portrayed the child Jesus with a mature face. Why would the artist do that? Do any of these stanzas carry the same idea? As you reflect, what kind of tune should this text have?

Sing the hymn. Is the tune sufficient?

The text takes us all the way back to 4th century Rome. It was written shortly after Christianity had emerged from the dark catacombs and persecution to become the official religion of the Roman empire. It was a time of flowering. Augustine was writing his sophisticated interpretation of the faith for the wise; Jerome was translating the Bible into Latin speech; Ambrose was recapturing singing for the common folk with "bewitched" folk tunes. The writer of this hymn, Prudentius, stepped into this circle of the great as the finest Christian poet of the time.

The text is rather unusual in its themes. Usually Christians turn to the First Person of the Trinity when they call for praise from creation. The grandeur of it all seems appropriate for God, the omnipotent Maker of heaven and earth. But Prudentius reverses procedures. All created beings are summoned to praise the Child of Mary. The poet suggests that the greatest glory of God is to be found in his "ungodly" state here on earth—when he was servant.

Perhaps the mood of the hymn, then, is well described by the 13th century plainsong. Somehow the claim for this God is made quietly, not grandly; with a deep joy and yet with a slight touch of poignancy—for the claim would be rather constantly ignored in history, where talk of power and even a powerful God dominates. The melody could be played by a wind instrument.

How many hymns in the hymnal summon creation to praise the Son?

Children of the Heavenly Father

Children of the heavenly Father
Safely in his bosom gather;
Nestling bird nor star in heaven
Such a refuge e'er was given.

In teaching this hymn, one must not lose sight of the warmth found in both the text and the music. The text never departs from the theme of God's grace and loving protection. Using the metaphor of the father-child relationship, the hymn alludes to God's complete satisfaction of our needs:

God his own doth tend and nourish,
In his holy courts they flourish.

The folk-like tune of this hymn cannot help but gain popularity among both young and old. Each of the four phrases uses the same rhythmic pattern, a pattern which in fact can be broken down into four notes (two eighths followed by two quarters). This four-note pattern repeats itself eight times within the four phrases of the hymn. Note that the first half of each phrase follows an ascending pattern, while the second half descends. There is another longer pattern also found in the hymn. The melody of the second phrase is pitched one step higher than the melody of the first phrase, and the melody of the third phrase is higher than that of the second. The last phrase takes us back down to the tonic note from whence we started. These simple devices make the tune both attractive and easy to learn. For this reason it is well suited for use with children, and they will love to sing it.

This hymn would fit into almost any season of the church year, lending itself especially to those days when the lessons speak of God's grace and love. It would, of course, be a fine hymn for a children's day service, and an excellent hymn for children to memorize. The simple lessons it teaches will remain with them for many years.

Jesus Shall Reign

Psalm 72 is the basis for this famous hymn by Isaac Watts. Introduce the text of the hymn by reading the psalm responsively by verses. The "king" in the psalm is prophetic or symbolic of Christ the King. Watts has given the Old Testament psalm a Christian emphasis.

On a chalkboard or large piece of paper make two columns. In the first column list the following psalm verses by number and perhaps one or two key words. Then read each stanza of the hymn with the group. Match each stanza with one of the psalm passages.

Psalm	Hymn
v. 5—sun, moon endures	s. 1
vv. 15, 17—long live prayer made name endure	s. 2, 3
v. 4—defend the poor, needy	s. 4
vv. 18, 19—blessed be God glory, Amen	s. 5

Discuss briefly the meaning of the hymn—a missionary hymn as well as a hymn of praise. The last stanza is a doxology uniting voices of earth with those of heaven in the "loud Amen."

The tune *Duke Street* is strong and full of energy. The musical direction at the top left indicates it should be sung "with breadth," not too fast. The half-note gets one beat, indicating a majestic rhythm. Keep strict time, with no extra value given to the whole note before the double bar.

This is probably a familiar melody. However, for those who may not know it, play the melody while the group listens. Then play the melody while the group sings the words. Add harmony when the group seems secure in the melody. For added interest for a familiar tune:

sing lines antiphonally—boys, girls; men, women;

sing one stanza without accompaniment;

add a descant*;

use an alternate harmonization.*

---

*See appendix.

Come, Thou Bright and Morning Star

This hymn of worship presents two or three problems to consider before a smooth, meaningful rendition of the hymn is possible. The problems are somewhat interrelated and have to do with tempo, meter feeling, and the text-music relationship. The crux of the matter is in the unfortunate fact that in a number of hymns (this one included) the musical phrases do not always lend themselves to the textual phrases. All too often the music has become the dictating element in singing, with the result that natural word phrases are broken up and we sing rather meaningless text snatches.

Use a tempo of about ♩ = 66. By using the half-note as the basic unit of pulse, it is very easy to move the melody along without a sense of "rushing it." The next suggestions relate to the meter feeling and text-music problems. Think and feel the music line in a 2/2—3/2 meter on the first (and repeated) line in this manner ♩ ♫♩ ♩ | ♩ ♩ ♩ | ♩ ♩ ♩ ♩ ♩ ♩ | ♩ 𝅝 :‖ —then go on to the last line with 2/2 feeling again. You will find that this suggests an easy, flowing line and a better syllable emphasis, particularly to the words in lines two and four of each stanza. One more reminder—keep the singing tone going at the ends of measures where the text thought continues. Example: stanza two—there should be *no break* or breath after "dew," "renew," or "store"—the tone should continue here until the word phrase is complete. In stanza three the singing line should continue to "works," and then a second phrase should continue to "joy." Let the text dictate the phrasing! One last comment—if the "Amen" is used, sing it in the same meter feeling as the rest of the song. Do not prolong it unnecessarily.

God's Word Is Our Great Heritage

Getting the music played *well* is the best way of introducing a new tune to a child. The music says something—something that really cannot be put into words. It ought to be played so well that it makes a sort of emotional impact on the child.

If there is not a good accompanist, it is probably better not to introduce the hymn in this way. It could then be sung by the teacher, or it could be played with one finger on the piano—but with movement and understanding. The way a song is presented will affect the child's desire and ability to learn.

The point is to get the children singing as soon as possible, with a minimum of talking. Getting more than half the group to sing is the battle and will give the whole group confidence.

This tune is to be played or sung with vigor; it is so good at the right tempo and so dreadful if sung too slowly. It is really a militant hymn.

The words are good, confidence-inspiring, timeless, a guide for any age.

Learning one stanza from memory makes it a part of you, and this should be encouraged. It then becomes a sort of word "hid in your heart."

There are gimmicks for teaching a difficult line and difficult intervals or for introducing new words. Such a word is "heritage," with two eighth notes on one syllable. It deserves a little special attention. It can first be said rhythmically, the teacher clapping or even stamping the rhythm, and then transferring this rhythm to the tune. The child delights in rhythm and loves this kind of drill. A response by the child can be assured through making the song alive rhythmically.

It is often a good idea to pick out phrases of some difficulty, "beginning at the end of the song" and "backing up" phrase by phrase to the beginning of the song. Then the song will be a delight for the child when he tries the whole stanza.

Out of the Depths I Cry to Thee

Motivation

Psalm 130 underlies this hymn. The theme of the psalm has, however, been somewhat expanded by Luther to make this one of his mightiest hymns. "He strikes chords which irresistibly compel the reader to pray, confess his sins, and trust in the Lord" (Ewald Schneider). This was a favorite funeral hymn in Reformation times. It was used at the funerals of Frederick the Wise, Elector of Saxony, and of Martin Luther, its author and the great Reformer of the church. It was one of the earliest hymns of the Reformation, written in 1523. It speaks to our depths and will help anyone express things to God for which he cannot find the words himself.

In preparing to teach this hymn, make a chart comparing this hymn with Psalm 130, in parallel columns. This should not be used at all when teaching the hymn.

Presentation

Words: What are the phrases that are hard to understand? (Note these on chalkboard.) Which words in each stanza summarize the stanza's meaning? Pick out some of the phrases from the hymn that unhappy people could use to express their sadness or anxiety. What phrases would help make the sad joyful? At what times in life would this hymn be especially useful?

Tune: Point out the repetition of the first line of music. Show the signs that indicate repetition. Sing each line for the group, pointing toward yourself while singing. Let word accents guide the accenting of the tune, though note values must be counted as written. Do not use an instrument at first. Add instrumental accompaniment only after the group has learned the tune.

Application

This hymn might be used in place of the reading of a psalm during a service, as a prayer of confession. It would be suitable for a funeral or a penitential occasion. Use for personal or family devotions, especially after a family quarrel, before Communion, and the like.

47

O God of Light

"O God of Light" is a hymn of only moderate difficulty, but one which is musically interesting because of its rich harmonic structure and the modulation to A major in the second line. To prepare the congregation or choir for the chromatic alterations in measures five, six, and seven, the organist should play through the hymn, using a strong registration but keeping the melodic line very clear. The melodic movement is primarily stepwise and stays within an octave.

In presenting this as a new hymn, the choirmaster or leader should make sure that his singers begin on *f#* and not *d*, the key-note of the hymn. The stanza ends on the root *d*, and it would be easy for singers to remember this pitch rather than the starting note.

The setting of the text presents a problem in clarity if the hymn is to be used for performance by the choir or for a broadcast where the words must be clearly understood. A new syllable appears on nearly every quarter note, and each must be clearly enunciated. Insist also that the text does not sound like, "O gah dove lye, thy wor da lam pun failing!" The standard advice to choral groups that they must "sing on the vowel" certainly applies to hymns such as this one, which have a considerable amount of rhythmic activity. To insure good diction, the text should be read through aloud at least once while preserving the rhythmic notation of the hymn.

As with many hymns, a simple but effective descant can be sung by a selected group of sopranos or played on a soprano instrument such as a flute or trumpet. The use of a descant is especially appropriate for festival days or a special program. It can add interest to the musical aspects of a hymn presentation at the same time serving to uplift the spirit as the descant soars above the melody.

It is interesting to note that this hymn was written in 1952 for the introduction of *The Revised Standard Version* of the Bible.

48

Alleluia, Song of Sweetness

Motivation

This hymn, a liturgical hymn, is particularly appropriate for Quinquagesima Sunday, although it can be used at any time during the pre-Lenten season.

The word "alleluia" is one of the most joyful and singable in the Christian vocabulary. From pre-Christian times it has served as an ejaculation of praise. Composers through the centuries have set it to music. In Gregorian chant the singing of the "alleluia" gave rise to the sequence which in turn led to countless hymns, the most famous of which is "Christ Jesus lay in death's strong bands" (SBH, 98), Luther's paraphrase of "Christ the Lord is risen again" (SBH 107), which in turn was a medieval German hymn based on the Easter sequence, "Christians, to the Paschal Victim."

The hymn speaks of the joy implicit in the word itself and of its temporary curtailment, a parallel for the Christian of his ultimate joy in heaven and the necessity to forego it for awhile on earth.

Presentation

It has become the custom, in deference to the emphasis on thoughtful preparation for Holy Week, to discontinue the singing of any alleluias during the season of Lent. The word disappears from the Propers from Septuagesima to Holy Saturday. On Easter and throughout Eastertide the alleluias pour forth in celebration of the resurrection. This hymn is a last celebration of the word before Lent.

This hymn might well be introduced by the children's choir singing it in unison.

Note the connection of the gradual and alleluia between the Epistle and Gospel—the gradual commenting on the Epistle just read, the alleluia looking forward joyfully to the Gospel.

Application

This hymn is appropriate for the Sunday service, church school, hymn programs, and meetings of parish auxiliaries. The adult choir might sing one or two stanzas in parts, as an alternate to congregational singing.

My Song Is Love Unknown

Students of all ages are intrigued by strange sounding names. Print the following list on the blackboard (at first without *Service Book and Hymnal* numbers):

393	*Aberystwyth*
230	*Ar Hyd y nos*
114	*Bryn Calfaria*
520	*Cwm Rhondda*
397	*Hyfrydol*
344	*Llangloffan*
65	*Rhosymedre*
343	*Rhuddlan*
547	*Ton-y-Botel*

These hymns constitute a little Welsh hymnal within a hymnal. This list might stimulate some research projects. The list could be used to introduce the Index of Tunes (page 999), Welsh Hymn Melodies (in the Index of Composers, page 995), and hymntune names, shown at the top of each hymn. Use your imagination to encourage student involvement in exploring the entire hymnal. Singing and interest will be improved if we take time to impart additional information.

In introducing this hymn, study Samuel Crossman's words. This hymn is undoubtedly one of the finest hymns on the Passion in the English language. But the poetic language is not simple. It takes some digging to discover just what Crossman is saying. Take special note of his references to events in the life of Christ: his birth, the miracles he performed, the event on Palm Sunday, his death. These events are beautifully pictured in the poem. And then note his conclusion in the last stanza.

It would be well to correlate the teaching of this hymn with the next Sunday service or a midweek service. Arrange something with the organist. A significant chorale prelude* by Vaughan Williams might be used to introduce the hymn.

One hymn can be the stepping stone to many usually unexplored but interesting and informative areas. Don't just teach the hymn assigned. Use it for the greater enrichment of the students.

---

*See appendix.

Ah, Holy Jesus

"Behold, the Lamb of God, who takes away the sin of the world!" In this hymn we are faced with the most tragic, and yet for man the most wonderful picture in all history: the Son of God suffering for the sins of humanity. The message of the *St. Matthew Passion* by Bach and the *Pieta* by Michelangelo is contained in the poignant hymn.

Read a portion of the Passion Story and discuss its meaning to us in the 20th century. View some pictures of the Passion by the masters and discuss the meaning of contemporary people appearing in many of these pictures as it relates to the line in the hymn, " 'Twas I, Lord Jesus, I it was denied thee: I crucified thee." Have the class listen quietly as you play the recording of the hymn from *A Time for Singing*. Point out the musical relationship between measures 1-4 and 9-12 as well as the inversion of the melody from measures 5-6 to 13-14. Hum the melody as the hymn is repeated either on a recorder *(block flöte)* or a keyboard instrument.

As was suggested above, this hymn can very effectively be coupled with visual presentation of the Passion Story, using slides, film strips, or reproductions of master paintings. It is, of course, a favorite Communion hymn. The Passion Story can be read while the congregation replies in litany-like responses using the stanzas of this hymn. The many fine organ* and choral* settings of this hymn might also be used in its presentation by the organ and the choirs.

In directing this hymn, beat two slow beats per measure instead of four.

Here is an interesting thought: Read the last line in each of the four stanzas consecutively. Taken together they form an interesting additional "stanza."

---

*See appendix.

Jesus, Name All Names Above

Albert Edward Bailey, author of *The Gospel in Hymns*, calls this hymn "one of the sweetest hymns of adoration in existence." In the world of today, where almost nothing is held sacred, it is important for us to learn and love and sing frequently a hymn which puts into words the feelings of awe and wonder which we have for our Savior.

Background

In one of the oldest parts of Istanbul are the remains of an ancient monastery called the Studium. Here in the ninth century several monks wrote prayers and poems in Greek which were used in the liturgy of the Eastern Church, and later were translated into metrical hymns by John Mason Neale, often called "the prince of translators." Actually, Dr. Neale was more than a translator. The original Greek (or Latin) with which he worked—in this case a "Suppliant Canon to Jesus" by a monk named Theoctistus—was usually a mere skeleton of thought to which the translator added expressive words of his own.

Music

This is a good chorale to teach to people who think they don't like chorales! Begin by having the organist play the melody, using 8' and 4' stops. Point out the simplicity of the tune, which moves only to the next note of the scale, either up or down. Have the congregation sing the first line on a neutral syllable, such as "la," at least twice. Then listen once again to the next line of music, pointing out that it, too, is a repetition—a two-measure phrase, then repeated a little higher. After the congregation sings this line on "la," have them finish the melody.

If time permits, give brief attention to the bass, mentioning that the bass in a chorale has an interesting melody of its own. Listen to the bass on the organ, or have the bass section of the choir sing it.

As the congregation now sings the hymn, be sure to have the choir sing the melody only. To show the beauty and intricacies of the harmony, you might have the choir sing one stanza in parts, with the congregation listening.

O Bread of Life from Heaven

Have you ever been hungry? Not many of us have had to stay hungry for long, but we all have known the feeling of spiritual emptiness that must be filled. The hymn "O Bread of life" expresses this yearning in words and music beautifully suited to each other.

The unknown author of these lines knew to whom he must go for relief from his spiritual hunger: to Jesus, whom he addresses as "the Bread of life, Manna from above, fount of grace, and river ever streaming." In the bread and wine of Communion he could know that Jesus hears his prayers and answers them, and not only his but the prayers of all those who seek him and hunger for righteousness.

The tune began as a humble folk song called "Innsbruck, I must leave thee." Bach said he would write his masterpiece on it, and he used it twice in the *St. Matthew Passion*. Mozart was powerfully attracted to it. Brahms composed the hauntingly beautiful chorale prelude, "O World, I Now Must Leave Thee," on this tune.

What is there about this simple melody that attracted such great musicians? While the organist plays it through, the singers might sing along on the syllable "loo." They could suggest some answers to the question. At least they would notice where the melody repeats, the small intervals which make it easy to sing, the expressiveness, the feeling of longing which is finally resolved in the last phrase.

To keep the quiet, yet flowing, feeling of the music, think of two beats rather than four to the measure, with no breaks in the time for breath marks. The ritard at the end intensifies the feeling of satisfaction expressed in the words and in the musical cadence.

The words of the second stanza might be appreciated more if this stanza were sung antiphonally. The six phrases could be divided one of these two ways: Group A sing phrases 1, 3, 4, and 6. Group B sing 2, 3, 5, and 6. Or Group A sing phrases 1, 2, 4, and 5, and Group B sing 3 and 6. For variation the third stanza could be sung (in unison, of course) to the accompaniment of Bach's harmonization found in Hymn 228, *Service Book and Hymnal*.

O Sacred Head, Now Wounded

This hymn can be taught very effectively to children, using a picture of the head of Christ as he suffered on the cross (e.g. Roualt's *Christ*). It is important that the children hear the tune a number of times before they try to sing it. This can be accomplished first of all by having it played on the piano while the children are coming into the room and as they are finding the hymn in the hymnal.

In a few words, explain that this beautiful hymn is especially suitable for the Lenten season and particularly for Good Friday. A very short discussion of Lent and Good Friday may be in order. Call attention to the picture and tell the children that they are going to learn a hymn which speaks of Christ as seen in the picture. Ask them to listen to the tune again while they look at the picture, trying to imagine what kind of poem they would write about it.

Ask them to read the first stanza together to see how the author of this hymn expressed his thoughts.

The leader, a child, or a group of children who have previously learned the hymn, may then sing a stanza or two. A recording may be used. Now ask the children to hum the tune as it is played or sung. If the piano is used, just play the tune without the harmony.

Next have them sing the tune on a "loo" syllable, encouraging them to sing with a light head tone.

Now have them sing by rote, repeating passages phrase by phrase after the leader. This may be necessary more than once. The next step is to have them sing it all the way through with only the tune played on the piano. The last step is to have them sing it alone, without any accompaniment, as a test to see if they really know the tune.

All Glory, Laud, and Honor

"All glory, laud, and honor" is, without question, one of our finest hymns and has been used widely throughout the Christian church, often as a processional hymn on Palm Sunday. It was written by Theodulph, a native of Italy, who was appointed Bishop of Orleans, in France, by Charlemagne. Being falsely accused of complicity during a rebellion, he was imprisoned. This hymn is possibly one of the many hymns written in a prison. One cannot help being moved by the thought of the "great cloud of witnesses" that have used this hymn in corporate worship. Hymns, as well as the liturgy, give a sense of continuity to God's people. It is one of the important reasons for keeping this legacy of the church alive and vital.

The tune is by Melchior Teschner (d. 1635), a Lutheran organist, choir director, and teacher. It was first published in Leipzig in 1615. Bach thought so highly of the tune that he used it in his *St. John Passion*. It is also used with the Advent hymn "O how shall I receive thee."

In the cathedrals of Europe, this hymn was often sung antiphonally, with the choir singing the stanza and the congregation singing the refrain. This practice might well be reinstated in our time, with choirs singing stanzas two through six and the congregation joining with the choirs on the refrain. If choirs can be located in different parts of the church, and each choir sings one or more stanzas, the effect can be most interesting. It should be noted, for this is confusing to some, that stanza one is repeated as a refrain following each of the stanzas two through six.

The English translation of this hymn was done by John Mason Neale in 1851. Neale adds the following interesting footnote: "Another verse was usually sung, till the 17th century, at the pious quaintness of which we can scarcely avoid a smile:

> Be thou, O Lord, the Rider
> And we the little ass;
> That to God's Holy City
> Together we may pass."

56

GOOD FRIDAY
Songbook—23
SBH—70

O Lamb of God Most Holy

This is one of the truly great hymns of the church, used most frequently during the Lenten season. It is a metrical version of the *Agnus Dei*, both text and tune written by Nicolaus Decius. Decius was a Catholic monk who embraced the Lutheran faith and became pastor of the St. Nicolas Church in Stettin, Germany. He was a popular preacher and a gifted poet, and seems also to have been a musician of some note. Luther prized this hymn so highly that he included it in his German liturgy.

An interesting introduction to this hymn might include a comparison with the *Agnus Dei* (SBH, pp. 36, 37, 64 or 65). The latter is sung or said each time Holy Communion is celebrated. How are the two alike? Where are the differences? Could the hymn version be used instead of the chant?

The melodic line of this hymn is easy to follow, and the text is readily understood. Children's voices sound especially appealing in this hymn since the melodic line and range is well suited to their flute-like voices, and they like to sing it. Children can easily sing it in two parts. The alto line is very simple. High school students or adults should sing it in four parts, though at least one stanza ought to be sung in unison, for it is the melody that is most outstanding. Though the second stanza is a repetition of the first, all three stanzas are always sung, as in the *Agnus Dei*.

If this hymn is one to be learned in the church school, this might also be a good time to learn one of the settings of the *Agnus Dei*.

The choral settings° of the hymn by F. Melius Christiansen and by Arnold Running are both attractive and one could be used as an alternate to the second stanza to give variety to congregational singing.

For the organist there are several very fine chorale preludes° available on this tune.

°See appendix.

That Easter Day with Joy Was Bright

This is a glorious Easter hymn. The tune *Puer Nobis* is an old plainsong melody which was made widely known by Michael Praetorius (1571-1621) who adapted it. Unlike so many hymns in the *Service Book and Hymnal,* there is no other use of this hymntune.

The words of the hymn are also of early origin, coming from Latin ancestry from as early as the fourth century. The text familiar to us was translated, edited, and adapted by John Mason Neale (1818-1866). The hymn is to be sung in unison. The opening words, "That Easter Day with joy was bright," describe how the hymn should be sung. Children love to sing these words, and the tune lends itself easily to even the very young. The hymn is probably sung as much as an anthem as it is as a congregational hymn. The choice stanza is surely the fourth. There can hardly be more eloquent yet simple testimony that God is alive and lives and reigns to all eternity. "To him all praise . . . we raise!" This hymn can be sung as a round with a fair amount of success, certainly well enough to be worth the try at an informal hymn sing. The second voice comes in four measures after the first voice begins. When time for preparation is available, minor adaptation of the second voice line permits a very smooth and delightful round or canon form.

Although this hymn is really suitable only for Easter Sunday (if one insists on literally interpreting the opening words "That *Easter Day* . . ."), it can be sung any time. This is also a fun song, and with the ease of learning the hymn and the ease of retaining the catchy triple meter melody, the hymn is a hit whenever hymns are sung, especially at song festivals, youth rallies, and the like.

58

Christ Jesus Lay in Death's Strong Bands

One of the neglected hymns of the Lutheran Church is this Easter hymn from the pen of Martin Luther. His inspiration came from the 11th century sequence hymn, *Victimae Paschali laudes,* still a part of the Easter liturgy in the Roman Church. For the music Luther borrowed a popular folk song for Easter. The result is a hymn of great strength and majesty.

Note the structure of the text. The first two stanzas review the life and death struggle between God and Satan during the days Jesus was in the grave. The third and fourth stanzas are a call to "keep the festival." Each stanza concludes with an exultant "alleluia."

Since these are not simple words, nor simple concepts, read the hymn carefully. Some review of the events of Good Friday to Easter may be necessary. Sometimes we forget what happened during the time Jesus was in the grave. Even then he was not a dead Savior. In the Apostles' Creed we confess that "he descended into hell." What a victory he won! What a Savior! Our alleluias should sound like trumpets!

The melody of this hymn is in a modal key. In no way does this make it somber or sad. Rather, it has a majesty and virility that somehow matches the greatness of the hymn's message and joyful faith.

Bach has added his rich harmony to give the melody buoyance and movement. There is a heartbeat that should not escape the singer.

Play the first line of music in a straightforward manner, not too slowly, and ignoring the fermata in mid-phrase.

Play again. This time ask your group to sing the melody, using the syllables du-ah, du-ah, etc., on each beat. Keep a steady rhythm. Sing the words in an equally rhythmic manner. Repeat for the other phrases. Practice the other stanzas in the same way, perhaps not all the first time. Save the final major chord *(tierce de Picardie)* for the very end. Play an F natural for the first three stanzas.

This will not be an easy hymn to learn. It may take more than a "once over" introduction to make it stick. Once learned, it will become a favorite in your storehouse of hymns.

The King of Love My Shepherd Is

If the leader says, "Today we will learn a new hymn; turn to number 530 and sing it," no one will be enthusiastic about singing. But let the leader suggest that this hymn is tender and beautiful in its simplicity, and if the congregation catches something of the tenderness and beauty of the melody to which the 23rd Psalm is set, everyone will be interested in singing it. It is the responsibility of the leader to set the stage, and create interest.

Psalm 23 is loved by every Christian. It is probably the favorite of both children and adults, including the old folks. It has been sung through the centuries to many different tunes and in many settings. The second tune in our hymnal is to a traditional Irish melody, and is perhaps one of the best. It is certainly melodic and singable by people in every age group.

To introduce the hymn, it might be well to say a few things about shepherds and sheep. Most people have seen sheep, but it is rare to find someone who has seen a shepherd. Since the point of Psalm 23 is the relationship between the shepherd and the sheep, this relationship must be explained. A picture, film strip, or story might be useful.

If the hymn is used at a church service or in a hymn festival, find ways of achieving alternation. Here are some suggestions:

1. Use a children's choir on the first stanza. The words are simple; children in grades one through three can sing them. Children have a way of reaching people with their innocent voices. If the hymn is new to the congregation, the children will break down the barrier quickly.

2. Have a young girl with a clear, unaffected voice sing the second stanza.

3. Let the congregation sing stanza three, perhaps with soft organ accompaniment.

4. Have all the children sing stanza four. The children should memorize the stanzas they will sing, perhaps even the entire hymn.

5. On stanza five, have everyone sing, again with soft organ.

For another variation, this hymn can be sung as a canon. The second group begins one measure after the first group.

Alleluia! Jesus Lives!

Every sermon recorded by the early church in the Book of Acts culminates in the story of the resurrection of our Lord. The disciples knew that everything in our faith hangs on what took place three days after Jesus died. The fact of that gaping hole in the garden broke like a new tide of hope upon his despairing followers. They thought all had been lost. Suddenly his risen presence was with them. The joy of that discovery caused all their speaking and writing to flow into the truth of his resurrection. Some of our greatest hymns testify to the joy of this great event. Someone has said that of the religions of the world it is only Christianity which has an extensive hymnody. The reason is that Christians have something to sing about, and all our joyous expressions are rooted in the proclamation of Easter morning.

The mood of this hymn is expressed in its first word, which is the English shout for the Hebrew word meaning "Jehovah be praised!" It is a word that need not be contained within the church's hymns on Easter Sunday. We live amid the smell of death, and our first impulse is to escape its reality. Anyone who has read Evelyn Waugh's horror-comic novel, *The Loved One,* sees a graphic description of how a vast business is built up to preserve us from taking a hard look at the meaning of death. In what way does the typical American funeral tend to cover over the reality of the grave? Is it possible to learn to hate life if we are possessed by the fear of death? Read Ecclesiastes 2:14-17 and contrast the preacher's words with Isaiah 26:19 and Psalm 73:23-26. Now read through the text of the hymn. Does the fact of the resurrection have something to do with the way we affirm our life here on earth?

This is an ideal hymn to sing antiphonally. Have the men sing the 1st and 3rd phrases, the women the 2nd and 4th, and everyone the 5th and 6th.

Holy God, We Praise Thy Name

An understanding of this great hymn of adoration can be gained by:

1. First reading Luke 2:14 (Glory to God in the highest).

2. Then reading the complete text of the 5th century Latin hymn *Te Deum* (Thee God We Praise). This may be found in any of the great choral works of that name, such as those of Berlioz, Bruckner, Verdi, and contemporary composers. The original text of this hymn, and the tune called *Te Deum* or *Grosser Gott,* are of unknown authorship, as is so characteristic of many hymns of Catholic origin. It contained eight stanzas in the first publication in the *Katholisches Gesangbuch,* Vienna, 1774. In our present translation only four have survived, though three more stanzas are published in *The Handbook to the Lutheran Hymnal* (Concordia Publishing House). These three stanzas make the *Te Deum* text complete.

3. Reading the seven stanzas side by side with the *Te Deum* text.

4. Then pointing out that this ancient text is ascribed to Nicetas, Bishop of Remesiana (now Serbia), though more probably it is a compilatio of several writers. This text has been used as a high point of praise in the service and as a national outpouring of thanksgiving to celebrate the end of war or a great victory.

Our hymn text is a translation by a Roman Catholic priest of Albany, New York, Clarence A. Walworth, who helped found the order of the Paulists in the United States.

The tune *Te Deum* may confuse some of our congregations because of at least four variants that have sprung up, the best known being *Hursley* (SBH 226). Compare the first sections of these two tunes and notice the far greater dignity and power of *Te Deum* in measures 2 and 4. The differences are seemingly slight, differences of cadence and passing notes, and a repetition in *Te Deum* that does not occur in *Hursley.* Yet even the musically uninitiated should be able to sense the greater strength of *Te Deum* as compared with a tendency toward sentiment in *Hursley.* Sing both tunes in unison, unharmonized by voice or organ, and then sing the tunes together, or have the organ play one and the congregation sing the other.

O God, Eternal Source of Love

Read the first two stanzas of the text. How wide is the grace hymned in the first lines? Is grace available in every gift? For the pagan as well as the believer? In the second stanza, do you see any difference between where we are called to serve and the place suggested in the refrain of No. 578 in the *Service Book and Hymnal?* On these questions hang great issues that confront the modern church.

No Lutheran should be without some acquaintance with Johann Sebastian Bach. Musicians from classicists to jazz enthusiasts find lines back to his genius. But Lutherans should know him because his music expresses so faithfully the essence of what Lutheranism is. Rarely, if ever, have faith and music been so perfectly wedded.

One marvelous quality of Bach is that each part in his harmonization has so much beauty of its own. Perhaps the group should play or sing each part alone to demonstrate its beauty. Then let all sing the hymn in unison to see how the harmonies support the melody.

Most choir directors race to prepare one anthem each week; Bach many times wrote the anthem for the coming Sunday. Since he carefully related his composition to the Gospel for the day, there is a tremendous Word-centeredness in his work.

It should be said, however, that Bach did not write original melodies. He took the great folk-hymns of earlier writers.

Johann Heerman, who wrote the text, was one of the greatest poets of German hymnody. His writings were forged in the fires of the Thirty Years' War of the early 17th century. His constant companionship with death and tragedy gives a quality of immediacy that makes his hymns deeply loved. But one also gets the strength of what he thought from his writing. God as the source of *all* knowledge and of *every* grace is only now being recovered in the life of the church (See Col. 1:17). Equally unusual is the insight of this stout old German that calling was to be lived out here—and this said in the midst of a war which might have prompted him to look constantly toward heaven as a place of escape from the weariness of life.

Look, Ye Saints, the Sight Is Glorious

" 'Look, ye saints, the sight is glorious' is undoubtedly the finest Ascension Day hymn in the English language" (*The Story of Christian Hymnody*, E. E. Ryden). Another of Thomas Kelly's hymns, "The head that once was crowned with thorns," in the *Service Book and Hymnal*, is likewise an appropriate hymn for this special day in the Church Year. It is unfortunate that Ascension Day is not generally celebrated in our churches because it falls on Thursday. Lest the scriptural witness concerning the ascension be forgotten, some reference to it can be made the following Sunday.

In teaching the hymn it may help to think of the rhythm in terms of 3/2 time, with three beats to the measure and a half note or two quarter notes receiving one beat. The music begins on the down beat. Note the repetition of "Crown him" in the third and fourth stanzas. We must sing the phrase six times in all stanzas rather than the four as printed in the text below the music. The last line in each of these same stanzas is repeated to fit the music. In the second line of the score, we can add a note of interest by dividing the singers into three groups: group I singing the first measure ("Crown him! Crown him!"); group II, the second; group III, the third; after which all may sing the last two phrases of the third line.

Thomas Kelly (1769-1854), the author of this hymn, was born in Dublin. Like Luther, it was while studying law that he decided to prepare for the ministry. Only after he comprehended the doctrine of justification by faith alone did he find peace of mind and soul. Because of his evangelical preaching he was finally forbidden to preach in any of the pulpits of the Anglican Church. He then became a Dissenter and erected places of worship. Besides being a magnetic preacher, he had extraordinary gifts as a hymnist. He wrote 765 hymns over a period of fifty-one years, and for many of them he also composed the music, thus performing the dual role of musician and poet. However, the musical setting for this hymn is not by Kelly; it is based on a Welsh tune.

Crown Him with Many Crowns

Who is the person to be crowned with many crowns? The Bible gives us the answer. (Read Revelation 5:13.)

The hymn writer describes this heavenly scene for us in the first stanza of our hymn. Let us read it together. (Group reads the first stanza.)

This hymn is a song of praise to the Lord Jesus. Each stanza tells us something about the kind of king Jesus is. Each stanza is based on something the Bible tells us about Jesus. We will list on our chart the name given to Jesus in each stanza. Then we will listen to the Bible passage which tells us why these titles can be given to Jesus.

Lord of life—John 1:4.

Lord of love—John 15:13.

Lord of peace—Ephesians 2:17.

Lord of years—Revelation 11:15.

Notice the second stanza. It reads almost like a story, for it tells of all that Jesus has done for us. This stanza was not written by the same man who wrote the other stanzas. It was written by Godfrey Thring, who was pastor of two small country churches in south-central England.

The writer of the other stanzas was also a pastor in England. His name was Matthew Bridges. You can find several other hymns by each author in our hymnal.

The tune for this hymn is named *Diademata,* a Latin word meaning crown or diadem. It was written especially for this hymn by George Elvey, a famous organist in St. George's Church in Windsor, England.

Several hymns in our church hymnal are sung to tunes written by George Elvey. Notice especially the one used for hymn number 91. Its name helps us to remember where the composer served as organist.

Come, Holy Spirit, God and Lord

"Come, Holy Spirit, God and Lord" is one of the oldest hymns in the *Service Book and Hymnal*. Its origin can be traced back to the 12th century sequence *Veni Sancte Spiritus*. Martin Luther adopted the German translation of *Veni Sancte Spiritus* and added two original stanzas, resulting in the three-stanza hymn we now use. The hymn was popular in Germany during the Reformation period and appears in many Protestant hymnbooks of the 19th and 20th centuries.

This hymn is excellent for introducing the plainsong tradition of singing in a smooth manner and in unison. Individual voice qualities should be well blended and the spirit of a prayer of supplication maintained. The women will sing at the notated pitch and men an octave lower. The choirmaster or organist should discourage men from singing two octaves below the melody as this results in a rather thick and plodding texture. The range of the melody is only an octave and one step, from middle C to fourth line *d*, so with some stretching it can be within the range of most singers. The melodic movement is primarily by step and uses small intervals. The only chromatic alteration of this melody is *b* natural in measures one and ten.

Fitting old music to modern notation usually results in a highly irregular rhythmic structure. The church musician must be aware of this problem and point out that not all measures have the same number of beats. The first full measure contains the equivalent of eight quarter notes, while measure two has four beats, and measure three has six! The important rule to remember is that the quarter-note pulse remains constant, no matter how many there might be per measure. The quarter-rest at the end of each line of text serves as a uniform breathing space and should be kept within the rhythmic context.

The eighth-note syncopations in measures seven and fifteen (lines four and eight of the text), should be clearly presented in the giving out of the hymn by the organist or in demonstration by a soloist or the choir.

Father Most Holy

This is a glorious hymn, one that is worthy of regular use. Through assigned to Trinity Sunday, it can be sung at any time, particularly throughout the Trinity season. It is a hymn that ought to be in the repertory of every congregation and every church school.

It might be well, in introducing the hymn, to point up and explain some of the phrases and terms used. For instance, it should be noted that each person of the Trinity is named in the first stanza and that one or more attributes of each person are given. Further, that in the second stanza the hymn is addressed to the Trinity as a triune God. Some words may need explanation too, especially when teaching the hymn to children. "Advocate" is one such word.

The tune is an 18th century French melody. It is a strong and very singable tune. Ralph Vaughan Williams (d. 1958), who arranged this setting, is well known in musical circles, and recently his hymn tunes and arrangements have become very popular in the church. He taught at Oxford University, England, and at the Royal College of Music. Among his compositions are several operas. But his name will be remembered most for such tunes as *Sine nomine* (No. 144, SBH), *Down Ampney* (No. 123, SBH), *King's Weston* and arrangements of this hymn and others, and for his work as musical editor of the *English Hymnal, Songs of Praise,* and *The Oxford Book of Carols.*

This hymn should be sung with dignity and joy. The tempo should not be rushed, but it must also not drag. Two slow beats to the measure (about m.m. 68) will give the right "feel" to the hymn. When leading the hymn, pay attention to the text, letting the text determine the phrasing. The music is only a vehicle for expressing the words more beautifully.

This hymn, like many hymns, concludes with an "Amen." The "Amen" should be sung in the same spirit and in the same tempo as the hymn. In this case, each syllable has two beats.

God Calling Yet

Motivation

Text and tune combine to recall the words of the Apostle Paul: "For the trumpet will sound, and the dead will be raised imperishable, and we shall be changed" (I Cor. 15:52b). But the change this hymn talks about is to take place before we die and before the great Judgment Day. The trumpet call of this hymn is to awaken the one who sings it to a life of regeneration in Jesus Christ. But the trumpet of Judgment Day and of eternity crackles in the background. "God calling yet."

Presentation

1. Note that the tune is like a fanfare which could be well played by a trumpet or a brass choir. It is crisp, but dignified.

2. Have the organ, piano, or some other bright instrument play the tune.

3. Ask the group to sing stanza one with the accompaniment.

4. Look at the words of the hymn.

a. Let the group suggest some key words for this hymn, words that set the mood and indicate the chief message.

b. Point to the almost physical "break" between stanzas 3 and 5; stanza 4 being an exhortation to yield God all. Stanza 5 is a violent breaking loose from the "earthly bonds." Note the decisive character of this hymn.

5. Check for words or phrases that may be obscure. Write them on the board and talk about them for clarification.

6. Sing the entire hymn with careful attention to the progression of spiritual action taking place within us as we sing it.

Application

1. How is this hymn similar to others, such as: "Softly and tenderly" (SBH 578); "Jesus calls us" (SBH 553); "Pass me not, O

gentle Saviour" (SBH 461)? (Use only one for comparison at a given time.)

2. What does this hymn say that makes it different from the others? Why is it better?

3. For what occasions would this hymn be helpful? Let the group discuss this a few minutes.

Built on a Rock

It would be difficult to imagine a stronger, more resolute hymn-tune than this. The composer, Ludvig M. Lindeman, was organist at *Vor Frelsers Kirke* (Our Saviour's Church) in Oslo, and a professor at the theological seminary there. He is credited with composing no less than six tunes found in the *Service Book and Hymnal*, and during his lifetime published a chorale book which collected and defined the hymnody of the Norwegian Lutheran Church.

Nikolai F. S. Grundtvig, who wrote the text, was an influential 19th century Danish theologian and poet. He has written seven texts found in the *SBH*, and has been called by one author "easily the greatest hymn writer of the period."

In teaching this hymn, one finds a wealth of material in the text to stress. It abounds in biblical metaphors which furnish us with a strong affirmation of God's church on earth and his presence in our lives. Compare if you will the brave lines of this text with the texts of many of our so-called Gospel hymns, which often seem to be little more than "frank excursions into sentimentality."

The tune of this hymn, with its angular movement and bold leaps, complements in every way the strength of the text. It uses only two basic rhythmic patterns, which are established in the first two phrases, and yet it drives forward with great vitality. It also has a climax note (a note which is higher than any other note in the tune) in the next to the last phrase, a musical feature lacking in many hymn tunes. This gives the melody a focal point, and tends to give the tune shape. Compare the strong melodic lines here with the jumping-jack sequences of the old hymn "Jesus calls us o'er the tumult."

This hymn lends itself to part singing if the accidentals can be sung in tune; otherwise a disagreeable distortion results. The text is appropriate for almost any season, especially Trinity, and would be particularly suited for the dedication of a new church.

70

All People That on Earth Do Dwell

The music is the "thing" in hymns—no matter what. This tune is probably familiar, at least to a majority. It is a tune of great dignity and such fun to sing as written in the *Service Book and Hymnal*.

Sometimes it is best not to use books. (The author of this page evidently has younger children in mind.—Ed.) Teach by rote if at all possible, the teacher singing a line and then the children. Swinging the arm for emphasis helps the children feel the rhythm. The rhythm is the key to the enjoyment of the hymn. Do not be afraid to clap the rhythm, or to tap it. Have the children clap with you. And then, within a pattern of the correct rhythm, drill the difficult intervals. The intervals will be learned much faster within this rhythmic pattern. Drill and drill the difficult ones, never missing a beat. This rhythmic repetition cannot be stressed enough.

This tune is not difficult and will need drill only for certain passages and for the words. Do not be afraid to *say* the words before singing them. Emphasize consonants as well as vowels.

Singing must be a happy experience; it must be made fun and alive. A teacher must love a hymn to make the children enthusiastic about it. He must also be sensitive to how much drilling can be done at a time. Music is a means and language of worship and not a performance; therefore the best is strived for as an offering, sincerely given. It takes a long time to perfect the singing of a hymn. If it is done correctly, the children will come back for more.

A song chart can be helpful for teaching. However, it should be used only as a prompter, for confidence, not to follow while singing. Eyes and ears must be open.

Occasionally instruments can add zest and spirit to the learning process. Even a string bass can add a beat to the rhythm of the song that delights the child. The trumpet is an exciting instrument for the church for special hymns and seasons. Add to these the flute, guitar, and percussion, if played well and artistically. We have ignored these props too long.

When the hymn has been presented so the child loves it, it will be a part of him forever.

TRINITY IV
Songbook—39
SBH—348

Turn Back, O Man

Motivation

1. This hymn is a call to self-examination and rededication.

2. It urges the Christian to live by the principle of brotherhood.

3. It emphasizes by contrast the temporality of earthly things and rulers with the eternity of God.

4. It is appropriate to seasons and services of preparation.

5. The tune has the nobility of the best of the tunes from the *Genevan Psalter*. It has breadth and sweep and rivals the German chorale in its sturdiness.

6. The *Genevan Psalter* consisted of the 150 biblical psalms, versified and set to music for congregational singing. In the thinking of John Calvin and his followers, only that which came directly from the Bible was good enough to be used in worship. Since other hymns were "of human composure," they were inadmissible. The result of this policy was that a substantial body of hymnody came into being, based on the Psalms. The best known of the tunes from this psalter, and quite possibly the best known hymntune in Western Christendom, is *Old Hundredth*, written by Louis Bourgeois and set to Psalm 100 for the *English Psalter*. It is most familiar to us as the setting for Bishop Kethe's doxology, "Praise God from whom all blessings flow."

Presentation

1. If new, introduce this hymn with the singing of the choir, in unison, giving it firm support, underscoring the solidity of both text and tune.

2 Point out and explain the half note "gathering note" at the beginning of each line. Used originally as a note on which to collect all the voices before moving on, it has become the hallmark of the psalm tune, lending it a peculiar dignity and deliberateness.

3. Sing it full and in unison with the congregation.

Application

1. It is appropriate for the Sunday service or for other morning or evening services, such as matins or vespers.

2. It would serve well as an example of a psalm tune for a program of hymns.

3. Use it in the setting by Gustav Holst, "Turn back, O Man,"* either as an anthem in the service, or as an extension of the hymn in the context of a hymn program.

---

*See appendix.

Lord Jesus Christ, Be Present Now

The authorship of this hymn is attributed to Wilhelm II, Duke of Saxe-Weimar, who in his student days devoted much time to the study of music and mathematics. Following his service during the Thirty Years' War, he seriously put himself to the task of restoring prosperity and piety to the people whom he governed. It was at this time that he was able again to study poetry and music.

In early hymnals this hymn bore the heading, "To be sung before the sermon." It became very popular, and according to the *Dictionary of Hymnology* by John Julian, "in 1678 was officially directed to be sung in all the churches in Saxony on all Sundays and festivals."

The translation of this hymn in the *Service Book and Hymnal* is by Catherine Winkworth. Miss Winkworth is regarded as the foremost translator of hymns from the German into the English language.

This hymn is in the familiar form of praise to the Holy Trinity which is summarized in the final *Gloria Patri* in verse form. This very obvious hymn for the beginning of the service or before the sermon can be used over and over again.

Congregations should be given the opportunity to learn the wonderful old rhythmic settings of the chorales where they are coupled with the better known metrical versions. This hymn offers us an excellent opportunity for comparing the original rhythmic version with the measured chorale as it was used in the time of Bach.

First, play the recording of the hymn from *A Time for Singing*. Next, play the record version (second tune) on the organ or piano, and then go back to tune one for the role of comparison. In tune one the quarter note value should be faster than in the Bach setting. The second tune uses a more stately tempo so that the changing harmonies and the passing notes are given a chance to bring out the marvelous coloring characteristics of Bach's setting.

Many organ settings on the tune for this hymn, *Herr Jesu Christ, dich zu uns wend*, are available.*

*See appendix.

74

Eternal God, Before Thy Throne We Bend

The creative effort of many centuries is represented in the *Service Book and Hymnal*. A well-planned hymnal will include not only the best from the past but also the work of contemporary authors and composers.

The words of this hymn are by the man who served as secretary of the Joint Commission on a Common Hymnal which prepared materials for the *Service Book and Hymnal*. This man also wrote the history of the hymns in our hymnal *(The Story of Christian Hymnody)*. What is his name? (Index of Authors, p. 991, SBH.) Show in the hymnal where authors are listed. Read the words of the hymn with the class. Ask the students to give names and adjectives that are used in the hymn. List on the blackboard three columns which could include the following:

Stanza 1	Stanza 2	Stanza 3
Eternal God	Lord	Spirit of truth
holy name	Jesus	Spirit of peace
grace	Christ	Spirit of joy
truth	Savior	flame of faith
righteousness	Friend	saving power
	love	
	Redeemer	
	Lamb of God	

After exploring the lists, the students should be led into the discovery of the trinitarian formula. Find other hymns that use the same outline.

The tune for this hymn was also written by a contemporary composer, Carl Landahl, who was a teacher at Augsburg College in Minneapolis until the time of his death. Show in the hymnal where composers are listed (Index of Composers, p. 995, SBH). When introducing the melody of the hymn, indicate the AAB structure. Encourage the students to fill out the half and whole notes (the white ones) with ample breadth of tone. For contrast, sing the hymn in a detached, choppy style; then with a smooth flowing line.

This is a hymn of praise—do not fail to observe the punctuation (every stanza ends with an exclamation point).

Jesus, Thou Joy of Loving Hearts

Does it inspire you to sing the song when you realize the labor, devotion, and genius which went into the creation of it?

Don't look at the hymn itself, but in ten seconds see what you can learn *about* it. If you're speedy you can find at least seven facts: (1) It is included in the section called "Contemplation"; (2) The name of the first tune is *Christe Redemptor* and the second is *Walton* or *Germany;* (3) L.M. means Long Meter; (4) William Gardiner included it in a hymnbook over 150 years ago; (6) Ray Palmer translated it; and (7) It is to be sung at a moderate tempo.

If you're curious and want to learn more, you can discover by looking in the index of the hymnbook that there are two more hymns set to the second tune of this hymn. Are they familiar? *Walton* is the name used in England and Canada, but *Germany* is perhaps the most common of its many names. It is called that because Gardiner insisted that it was from somewhere in the works of Beethoven, and Beethoven was a German. Lowell Mason considered it so "delicate and chaste a tune that it required too finished a style of performance to be used as a common church tune."

The original Latin poem of fifty stanzas inspired David Livingstone as he wandered in the jungles of Africa. He called it the hymn on the Name of Jesus. The translation we have is by far the most popular of the many that have been done.

More inspiring than information *about* it is the song itself. Let's listen to it, using the second tune. Words and music alike are deeply devotional, confident, and pleasant. The meter contributes to the even-tempered feeling because it is perfectly regular. Notice how each phrase of four measures begins on an upbeat. Do you feel the upsurge of emotion in the last two phrases as the melody rises higher and higher?

Love and devotion to their Lord inspired the writers of this hymn. We can show our love and devotion by our wholehearted singing.

An organ prelude by Garth Edmundson on *Germany* is included in *Seven Classic Preludes on Old Chorales.**

---

*See appendix.

Our God, to Whom We Turn

People seem to have definite feelings about the hymntunes which fall into the "chorale" category. There are those who dislike chorales with a passion on the grounds that chorales are difficult to sing. There are others who have a firm conviction that chorales are the only real "Lutheran" hymntunes and should be used almost exclusively.

It is often easy to convince the first group that chorales are both singable and beautiful. The people in the second group often cause more trouble in teaching a chorale, for they are prone to hang on to each note for dear life, dragging out each phrase interminably. This can kill a good chorale. So . . .

Rule #1: Don't drag it. Keep the tempo moving. A straight, deliberate, moderate tempo is best.

Rule #2: Stick with the melody. We have here a beautiful harmonization by the music master himself, J. S. Bach, and it may sound like musical heresy to say, "Don't use it." That, of course, is not what we are saying. Let the organ provide the harmony. The organist may well use a different harmonization on one or two stanzas, after the congregation is familiar with the chorale and knows the melody well. Make the congregation sing the melody strongly. Try using a neutral syllable, such as "la," until they are thoroughly acquainted with the tune.

Another use of the harmony might be to have the choir sing one stanza in parts, a cappella. (It would not be too fitting to use stanza three in this manner, since it speaks directly of the organ.)

Rule #3: Don't neglect the words. This is a beautiful chorale, but don't get so wrapped up in it that you let the congregation forget the importance of the words. Words such as these can have special portent and meaning for us in today's uncertain age. God is the one sure refuge, the only enduring Eternal, in this world of confusion and constant change. Let us sing this hymn with faith and all the strength at our command. And in this singing we will find further strengthening of that faith.

Take My Life, and Let It Be Consecrated

This is a good hymn for children because of its pictorial text. It would be very good during a missionary emphasis in the church school. With small children the use of bodily movements to portray the text would be interesting and would create interest for them.

The life story of Frances Ridley Havergal would be an interesting introduction to this hymn. Miss Havergal is often called "the consecration poet," partly because so many of her hymns are hymns of consecration, and partly because she so fully lived her hymns. Dr. E. E. Ryden, in his book *The Story of Christian Hymnody*, says, "To read the story of her life is not only an inspiration, but it discloses at once the secret of her beautiful hymns." Writing about her deep religious experience at the age of fourteen, she said, "I committed my soul to the Savior, and earth and heaven seemed brighter from that moment." Her prayer, in this hymn, "Take my silver and my gold; not a mite would I withhold," was not idle words. She did just that.

In presenting the hymn, it should be noted that most of the tune is diatonic melodic movement. The downward skip of a sixth in the fifth measure should be watched to make sure that it is sung accurately. Some of the words in the text will need explanation so that children may more fully enjoy singing this hymn.

Children love the use of instruments with the music they sing. Use whatever instruments are available. A clarinet would be effective with this hymn. Have the clarinetist play the tune through once or twice, then have the children sing along with the clarinet. For variety have the children sing the melody and have the clarinet play the alto line. In this way something special is made of the hymn while at the same time the children learn a new hymn.

78

Love Divine, All Loves Excelling

The approach to teaching this hymn is for the whole congregation on Sunday morning. Almost everyone has sung this fine text, but for many the first tune *Hyfrydol* may be new. (For other suggestions concerning Welsh tunes, see hymn No. 65, SBH, page 49.)

The hymn may be taught before or after the service, depending upon when it will be used. If the hymn is to be used that same day, it should be taught before the service. If it is being taught a week or two in advance of its use, then a rehearsal at the close of the service seems most logical.

Although there are some who object to a rehearsal in connection with a worship service, the fact remains that this is the only time that the majority of the congregation is assembled so that an effective rehearsal can take place.

It is very important that the choirs have learned this hymn before it is taught to the congregation. It is also helpful to have taught the hymn at organizations such as Women of the Church, Luther League, etc.

To teach the hymn it is very effective to use a choir in the front of the church, facing the congregation. Ask the congregation to turn to hymn No. 397, the first tune. Say only three or four enthusiastic sentences about the new tune and familiar text they are going to sing. Ask the congregation to follow the hymn in the hymnal as the choir sings it. After that ask the congregation to sing line by line after the choir with some kind of accompaniment support. After going through the first stanza in this manner, repeat the process on the same stanza, but without accompaniment. If they do not start out well, stop them, give them a little encouragement, and start again. Often just asking them to sit up and hold their books up will help the singing a great deal. If they have trouble with any spot such as the run in the last line, demonstrate it once and ask the congregation to sing it over several times. Go back and have the congregation and the choir sing the whole stanza and as much more of the hymn as time-permits.

Jesus, Priceless Treasure

The author of this hymn, Johann Franck (1618-1677), lived much of his life during one of the most difficult and devastating periods of German history—the Thirty Years' War. Against this background of political, social, and religious upheaval, the expression of utter confidence in Jesus Christ and the resultant peace and joy of the believer is even more remarkable. The spirit of the text is intensely personal, and anyone singing this hymn without the appropriate commitment may well find himself embarrassed and ill at ease in the presence of such religious fervor. It has been translated into many languages, including Russian, and has been included in a number of contemporary non-Lutheran hymnals.

Franck's famous hymn was published in the 1656 edition of Johann Crüger's monumental collection of chorales, *Praxis Pietatis Melica*. When one notes that no less than nine different Crüger melodies are included in the *Service Book and Hymnal*, the importance of this 17th century German musician is firmly established. In addition to "Jesus, priceless Treasure," Crüger is also credited with such universally respected tunes as those for "Now thank we all our God," and "Deck thyself with joy and gladness."

The wedding of text and tune in "Jesus, priceless Treasure" is beautifully realized. As a result, there are no particular problems of execution. This chorale was a particular favorite of J. S. Bach who used it as the basis for his motet, *Jesu, meine Freude*. This motet has been sung by generations of students in college and university choirs throughout our country. The use of this hymn in congregational worship will undoubtedly evoke a very special response from those who have sung the motet as well as from those who have heard it sung. A good recording of the motet would be a wonderful addition to any church library. In fact, a study of Bach's musical exegesis of the text might prove most helpful and inspiring to the perceptive song leader. The organist should be encouraged to use one of the Bach harmonizations of the chorale as a prelude to the hymn.*

---

*See appendix.

My God, How Wonderful Thou Art

If ever there was a hymn that was a revelation from heaven and a direct gift of God, surely this is the hymn. It is short, simple, pure, and intense, a beautiful expression of worship. The tune *Dundee* (French) which comes from the *Scottish Psalter* of 1615 is also used for the Holy Communion hymn "According to thy gracious word" (SBH 266). The hymn is found in many youth choir music books and is so simple that any age group can learn it readily.

The text is by Frederich Faber (1814-63). Faber was born an Anglican but became an adult convert into the Roman Catholic Church. All of his 150 hymns were written after his conversion. Of these, eight can be found in the *Service Book and Hymnal*. Many of his hymns have been edited for Protestant use, and among them are hymns dearest to the hearts of Christians of all denominations.

In most of our hymns we either pray *to* God for blessings and gifts or praise him for his majesty and unbounded love. In this hymn, however, we additionally think *about* God. The first four stanzas express God's glories with imagery rather clearly drawn from the Book of Revelation. The last three stanzas suddenly become intimate, expressing God's tenderness and love to us, his sinful children.

Originally this hymn appeared in Faber's *Jesus and Mary* (1849) with eleven stanzas. While most contemporary hymnals reduce the number to four or five, the *Service Book and Hymnal* includes the seven choice stanzas.

Because of its simplicity, it makes a fine solo and can be sung that way for variety. The hymn makes an appropriate and deeply felt prayer, a fine basis for one's own private devotion or as a regular part of a family's daily devotion. Certainly this hymn, in a most unusual way, is an expression of the universal language of religion, used and understood by all races and creeds.

Holy Spirit, Truth Divine

All of us are familiar with the name Henry Wadsworth Longfellow. We know that he was a great American poet. But how many of us know that he had a brother, Samuel, who wrote some beautiful hymns? Two of his hymns are in our hymnal.

Samuel Longfellow served congregations in Fall River, Mass., Brooklyn, N.Y., and Germantown, Pa. The last years of his life he spent in writing the life story of his famous brother poet.

Longfellow's hymn "Holy Spirit, truth divine" is really a prayer addressed to God, the Holy Spirit. Each stanza of the hymn helps us to understand how the Holy Spirit helps us to believe and to live as children of God. It makes us think of the explanation of the Third Article of the Apostles' Creed. We know that it is only by the Holy Spirit's help that we can come to faith in God.

The man who wrote the tune for this hymn was Orlando Gibbons. He was born in England on Christmas Day in 1583. He became a famous musician and wrote many anthems and hymntunes. Four of his hymntunes are used for hymns in the *SBH*. In his later years Gibbons was appointed organist of Westminster Abbey where he served two years. He lies buried in Canterbury Cathedral.

Beside the name of the tune we often find some letters or numbers. These refer to the meter of the hymn. The numbers indicate the number of syllables in each line. Such information is needed to make sure a tune will fit the hymn for which it is chosen.

"Holy Spirit, truth divine" is a good hymn to use as a prayer. Each stanza can be used by itself. The first stanza may be prayed before reading or studying the Bible. Stanza three is a prayer in which we ask for strength to live as God wants us to live. Stanza five may be called a prayer for guidance.

In presenting this hymntune for the first time, the melody can be patterned by an instrument such as a flute or an oboe. Also, the hymn can be used very nicely unaccompanied.

Open Now Thy Gates of Beauty

This is one of the "older" hymns which very likely many members of the congregation know. It is good to call special attention to some of these in an attempt to renew interest and enthusiasm. In our desire to teach new hymns, we sometimes tend to neglect those which are precious to many members of the congregation.

The author of "Open now thy gates of beauty" was a 17th century German Lutheran pastor, Benjamin Schmolck. He was well known as a preacher and pastor but was most popular for his devotional books and hymns. He is credited with the authorship of some 900 hymns.

The name of the tune for this hymn is from the composer, Joachim Neander. He is also well known as the author of one of our most famous hymns of praise, "Praise to the Lord" (SBH 408).

In the presentation of this hymn, it would be good to introduce it by an unaccompanied trumpet or cornet solo. Have everyone sing the first stanza with full organ and with the trumpet or cornet playing the melody.

Stanza two may be sung by only the women's voices accompanied by organ.

Following stanza two the organist might modulate to the key of B flat and the next stanza could be sung by only the men at a somewhat slower tempo. If the congregation is unaccustomed to tempo changes, this should be indicated on the church bulletin or special insert. The organist, however, can prepare for the tempo change during the modulation.

After the organist modulates back to the key of C, have only the children sing stanza four at the original tempo.

The last stanza should be grand and majestic. Have everyone, including all choirs and congregation, sing this in unison accompanied by full organ and trumpet.

Particularly fine organ chorale preludes on the tune *Neander* are included in *The Parish Organist,** Part 2 and *Ten Chorale Improvisations,** Op. 5 by Paul Manz.

---

*See appendix.

Immortal, Invisible, God Only Wise

It is good for us to sing a hymn that extols the majesty of our praiseworthy God. Too often we have allowed our worship of God to be familiar and even chummy. The Hebrew people will not so much as speak the sacred name for God. His accessibility and nearness so dramatized by the coming of Christ should not prevent us from hallowing his name in all its wisdom, power, and glory. This hymn raises our voices to praise his sublime majesty. The text reminds us we do not stroll leisurely into the presence of God with our hands in our pockets and an idle look on our face. In this hymn we are worshipers, dazzled by the perfection of his glory.

This is a contribution to our hymnody from the Reformed tradition. It was written by a great leader of the Scottish Presbyterians, Sir Walter Chalmers Smith. The tune is a Welsh air taken from a popular folk song of the early 19th century. Welsh hymns are some of the strongest in Christendom. It was not too long ago that they were first discovered and used widely because of the isolation of their dialect and church life. All Welsh songs are virile and powerful expressions of faith as they would have to be to capture the interest of great numbers of sturdy miners from the coal fields of Wales. The Welsh people love to gather for all-day hymn-fests, and this particular hymn is one of their favorites. It is said that if a person is allowed to witness one such hymnfest, he will never again treat his hymnbook casually or allow his voice to participate only half-heartedly in the praise of God.

Dr. Smith suggested he wrote this hymn from his study of I Timothy 1:17. Read the sections of Scripture that describe God revealing himself to Moses in the commandments (Exodus 19:16-23; 24:12-18). What feeling do these passages give you? Are there evidences today that reverence is not an important quality of our praise to God? Why? Read the last stanza of this hymn together and explain its meaning. As an aid in emphasizing its meaning sing this hymn by varying the volume at different points according to your interpretation. For example, the first two lines of the second stanza could be sung with hushed voices, building to a crescendoing climax in the last stanza.

All Glory Be to God on High

The inspiration of this hymn was obviously the *Gloria in Excelsis,* Luke 2:14. The hymn is the metrical version of the *Gloria in Excelsis* normally used in the liturgy. In fact, the *Service Book and Hymnal* suggests that on occasion this hymn might be used in place of the non-metrical version.

Nikolaus Decius, who wrote the metrical version in 1522, was a Benedictine monk who had become a part of the Reformation movement. This hymn was the first outburst of great music to grow out of the Reformation. It preceded Luther's first hymn by at least a year. Popular preacher, gifted poet, Decius is also credited with the tune for the hymn, though there is some doubt about this.

The basic idea developed in the hymn is the Trinity. In presenting the hymn, read Luke 2:14 first, then the text of the *Gloria in Excelsis* from the liturgy, followed by lines 1, 5, and 6 in the first stanza. Call attention to the development of the basic idea as it is presented in the hymn, particularly in stanzas 2, 3, and 4. An analysis of the different functions of the Father, Son, and Holy Ghost might be made. Rarely is theology so clearly set forth in poetry. Each of these stanzas is a priceless sermon, complete in itself, but with a special meaning when studied together. The translation is by Catherine Winkworth, who did so much to bring great German hymns to the English speaking world.

The tune, which did not appear until 1539, was derived from Gregorian chant. It has considerable strength in triple rhythm, but it might be interesting in some groups to sing it in duple meter too.

This hymn is to be sung "joyfully; with breadth." It is a strong hymn and cannot be sung sentimentally. If instruments are used with this hymn, they ought to be brasses.

Many excellent organ settings of this hymn have been published.* When the hymn is used at a Sunday service, the hymn might be introduced in the prelude by using one of these settings.

---

*See appendix.

Awake, My Soul, and with the Sun

Bishop Ken began each day with this stirring hymn of his own writing. He sang to his own accompaniment on the lute as a part of his private morning devotions. The words call to mind the verse from the Old Testament, "Arise, shine; for thy light is come."

Thomas Ken (1637-1711) was one of the earliest writers to make the transition from psalmody to hymnody. A little research on this development will prove interesting and helpful to the teacher. He apparently wrote only three hymns. Be sure to become acquainted with his evening prayer, "All praise to thee, my God, this night"; his midnight hymn, "My God, now I from sleep awake," as well as the morning hymn we are discussing here. All three hymns end with the familiar doxology, the most famous stanza of its kind ever written, "Praise God, from whom all blessings flow."

Born in England in 1637, Ken was left an orphan in early childhood. He was brought up by his brother-in-law, the famous angler, Isaak Walton. During his many years in the service of Charles II as chaplain, he revealed a spirit of boldness as he discharged his duties as spiritual advisor of his king. As his body was lowered into its last resting place, and the first light of dawn came through the chancel window, his friends sang his morning hymn as had been his custom throughout life.

Unless sung with spirit and movement the lyrics will be robbed of their inherent zest. While a short catch breath is permissible at the designated points in the hymn, it is at the double bar where we stop to fill our lungs so that we can proceed with smooth vigor. This can be achieved by holding the half note before the double bar only one beat and regarding the second beat as a quarter rest during which the singer takes a deep breath.

It is interesting to observe that the hymntune is named *Morning Hymn*.

In Christ There Is No East or West

In the decades since its writing, this hymn has become one of the most popular of our missionary hymns. John Oxenham wrote it originally for the "Pageant of Darkness and Light" sponsored by the London Missionary Society in 1908.

The hymntune was composed somewhat earlier by Alexander Reinagle, who named the tune St. Peter for the church where he was organist: St. Peter's-in-the-East, Oxford. The tune practically sings itself. Its uncomplicated scale-wise sequences, gentle leaps, and straightforward rhythm will make it easy to learn. If not already familiar, play the melody several times. Have the group hum the tune, then sing the words.

Here is a hymn where the importance of the text might be emphasized with visual interest. Several suggestions follow.

1. Add a figure of Christ to a map of the world.

2. Place a picture of Christ in the center of a large piece of paper or flannel board. Surround the figure with faces and figures of people of various nationalities and vocations. (Picture magazines are good sources.)

3. Make a picture display of missionary work of The American Lutheran Church. Mark the areas on a map.

4. Discuss the meaning of the words. Let each one in the group draw a picture of his idea of the hymn.

5. Act out several stanzas of the hymn (particularly 1, 3, and 4). Four children could be east, west, north, and south. Others in the group could be the "one great fellowship" and "brothers of the faith." Let the children decide how they might like to illustrate the meaning. While half the group "acts," the other half might sing the hymn, or speak the words as a choric reading.

6. Use a slow, sweeping hand motion in an arc form on each phrase. This will not only indicate the breadth of the musical phrase, but will also underscore the scope of the text.

Praise to the Lord

This hymn is to be sung majestically. That is the way most people have sung it since Bach's time. The argument for the slow pace is that it gives dignity and solemnity to the words. How do you react to such a way of indicating dignity? Do you think the tune should be heavy and sonorous or light and airy? At times the opening two lines, sung more rapidly, can sound like crackling flames, leaping to praise God.

"Praise to the Lord" ranks as one of the great chorales of the church. Fortunately the words do not suffer in translation. It was composed toward the end of the great period of Germany hymnody —from Luther's time to the end of the 17th century. Do you think it is as strong as "A mighty fortress"? It does not suffer too much in comparison with the greatest, but Pietism, a movement in Lutheranism, was beginning to work at the chorale. Its warmth did much for Lutheranism in a bitter time, but in the end it sentimentalized the chorale and dissolved it into inwardness.

Joachim Neander, the writer of the text, after a profligate life, became an adherent of Spener, the father of Pietism. In the last years of his brief life he wrote no less than fifty-seven fine chorales and twenty original tunes. A person of some eccentricity, he spent much time in natural settings, including a cave named after him. Many of his hymns are occupied with praise from nature and from the people of God.

Praise is a word that occurs in the Scriptures, particularly in the psalms, over and over. There are times when all things and all men scripturally seem to be dancing with joy before God, in ecstasy drawing "all that hath life and breath" into the celebration. Read Psalms 145-150 to hear how this hymnal of the Old Testament ends in a whirling motion of celebrators singing "Praise God!" What other hymns besides this one have this flavor? Have you ever read a piece of literature or seen a movie or a painting that reflects this praise? What if every meditative moment were to be used to wrest from incident, person, or thing a reason for praising God!

Deck Thyself with Joy and Gladness

Lay activity in the church has increased greatly during the last decade or more. This is as it ought to be. This hymn was written by a layman, Johann Franck, who was born in Guben, Germany, in 1618. His father was a lawyer. He studied law at the University of Königsberg, returned to his native city to practice law, and later became the mayor of the city. His interest in the writing of hymns was stimulated by his friendship with hymnists such as Simon Dach and Heinrich Held. He is ranked as second only to Paul Gerhardt among the hymn writers of his time.

This hymn, particularly suited for the celebration of Holy Communion, expresses hope and assurance in a spirit of quiet humility. It is perhaps the most commonly used hymn at Communion, and is placed first among the Communion hymns in the *Service Book and Hymnal.*

In singing the hymn, there should be easy movement in the melody, with no sluggishness. The pulse feeling should be that of the half note in a tempo of about $\quad = 76-80$. The text should dictate the phrasing; most of the phrases being two or three measures in length. In stanza two, however, the final two lines (those after the repetition) should contain four and six measures, respectively. The singing tone carries along throughout the complete word phrase in each case. Always let the music accompany the text. Do not force the text to fit a musical form at the expense of continuity of thought.

It should be noted that there is a meter change in the second score of the hymn (the four measures following the repeated section). These four measures should follow a rhythmic pulse thusly: that is, triple feeling in the first and third measures, duple in the second and fourth (1-2-3, 1-2-3; 1-2, 1-2, 1-2; 1-2-3, 1-2-3; 1-2, 1-2, 1-2), with the tempo of the underlying quarter note remaining constant throughout. The final score returns to the meter of the first score.

Excellent organ and choral settings* on this hymn are available.

---

*See appendix.

Lord, Keep Us Steadfast in Thy Word

Motivation

"A hymn for children" is the heading that Martin Luther gave this hymn written in 1541. It was written at a time when war threatened, and a special service of prayer for the nation's protection was held. Choir boys first sang the hymn at that service.

It is a prayer to the Triune God. When we sing it, we ask for God's mighty spiritual weapons to defend Christ's people in this world. We pray for deliverance from the ravages of war and the dangers of ungodly international movements and policies. We trust in God for this. But we pray for inward personal strengthening too, and this prayer asks for divine support that continues beyond this present life, but will lead "out of death to life." Let's look at this simple hymn with its mighty message for a riddled, anxiety-ridden world. May it lead us to the God of might and effective deliverance!

Presentation

1. Look at the words a few minutes. Have the group find the words and phrases that elicit faith in God.

2. Look at the melody. Point out that this is a "melody" hymn. Learn it without an instrument. Reformation congregations sang it without accompaniment, and it could well be sung in this manner today.

3. The melody must be kept moving and legato. Emphasis should be given, not to each individual note, but to the climaxes. The main climax is in the third phrase of the tune, at the words of the first stanza: "Would wrest the kingdom . . . ," with the accent coming on the syllable "king" in "kingdom."

4. When the tune has been learned, sing all stanzas with accompaniment.

Application

In Sunday school, the means by which God gives the answers to this hymn-prayer might be illustrated: How are those curbed, who by craft or sword would wrest the kingdom from the Son? How does the Lord Jesus Christ make his power known? How does the Comforter send peace and unity on earth? This could be a project on the church. This could lead to social service projects of obedience to the Lord who calls us to labor with him as he answers this prayer hymn. It is obviously useful for festivals of the church and at times of national crisis.

Ye Watchers and Ye Holy Ones

This popular hymntune, which first appeared in 1623, was originally set to the Easter text *Lasst uns erfreuen,* hence the designation of the tune by that name. The text of the hymn was based by its author largely on texts from ancient Greek liturgies, the second stanza in fact being a paraphrase of the Theotokian hymn sung at the close of the Eastern choir offices.

Repetition in the melody of a hymntune makes it easier to learn. Only when such repetition becomes tiresome, when it is done over and over again, is it bad, as in the old chestnut, "Blest be the tie that binds." Such a tune has no propulsive feeling. It does not move anywhere. It seems rather to be a dissertation (or perhaps dissipation) on the interval of the third, ascending and descending. Now compare our tune *Lasst uns erfreuen* with "Blest be the tie." Our tune is certainly crammed with repetition, indeed each phrase is sung twice. But what strength is found in this melodic repetition! The tune moves. It utilizes the whole scale. It is not fixed on any single melodic interval. The melody is made up mostly of stepwise motion, and when a skip appears within a phrase, it is crucially placed. The harmony is straightforward and, with few exceptions, diatonic rather than chromatic. Chromaticism in a hymn often tends to weaken the fiber of the music. A good hymntune may have chromatics in it, but it will not rely upon them for specious attractiveness. And finally, the tune here is rhythmically exciting. It propels itself onward.

The alleluias in the refrain can be sung antiphonally, with the choir and congregation alternating on phrases, or with two choirs singing them from different locations in the church, or perhaps the choir and congregation alternating with instruments. All would join on the final alleluia. The hymn is useful for any festive day or season, and is surely a favorite in many Lutheran congregations. It would not, of course, be used during Advent or Lent.

Guide Me, O Thou Great Jehovah

"Guide me, O thou great Jehovah" can be sung and performed in a variety of ways because of its straightforward rhythmic movement, simple harmonic structure, and the diatonic melodic line which spans only one octave.

The first four measures are closely related to the second four. It is effective to emphasize this similarity, but add variety to the hymn by using only male voices on the first phrase and answering this with the women on the second phrase. The last six bars could be sung together in four-part harmony.

The tenor and alto voice lines are fairly simple. Many pitches are repeated and most of the movement is by step with only a few leaps. Interesting but uncomplicated movement in the soprano and bass parts helps to make this hymn excellent for unaccompanied singing by a choir of even modest ability.

The last line of text is repeated. Its first appearance has five eighth-notes, each with a different word or syllable. Emphasis must be placed on clear pronunciation to keep the text understandable. The consonants of the last two lines of the second stanza are particularly troublesome: "Strong deliverer be thou still my strength and shield." All parts must keep the eighth-notes in strict tempo so that they are neither rushed nor dragged out.

The regular rhythmic movement and strong voice lines make this hymn well adaptable to the use of brass instruments. Two trumpets and two trombones or baritones would provide an effective accompaniment for choir or congregational singing. The music for trumpets in B♭ must be transposed one whole step higher than the original notation. If a baritone is available and the performer reads bass clef, this is generally a more satisfactory bass instrument than the tenor trombone. French horns could be used on either the alto or tenor parts if transposed up a perfect fifth. The brass need not be used on each stanza as more effective singing will result from a change in texture.

Shepherd of Tender Youth

Historical writings show us that the Christian church began to use hymns and spiritual songs at a very early date. These hymns were not necessarily taken from the Psalms. "Shepherd of tender youth" is such a hymn. Dr. E. E. Ryden, in his book *The Story of Christian Hymnody*, refers to it as "the oldest Christian hymn." The original Greek from which this hymn was taken was written around the year 200 A.D., by Clement of Alexandria. The translation which we usually sing (by Henry Martyn Dexter) often causes us to think of this hymn in terms of children and young people. But this was not the intent of the original Greek, which is translated literally as "Bridle of colts untamed." The author seems to have been writing for the instruction of people who were recent converts to the Christian faith. Clement was himself an adult convert to Christianity, and it was only natural that he would give thought and emphasis to the education of others.

When introducing this hymn, it would be interesting to mention its ancient origins. Facts on the background of hymns often perk up interest among the learners, and therefore make it easier to teach and learn the hymn.

Attention must be given to the words of this hymn. If you are teaching it to children, several of the words should be explained, such as "devious," "hither," "abase," "trod." The ideas and meaning of each stanza will need explanation, too, but be careful not to do too much explaining and too little singing!

After you have been working with the hymn for a while, stop and ask the children what words they do not understand. You may be amazed. Many words which we take for granted because we have sung them for years are like an entirely foreign language to our children.

The melody is easily singable. After a little preliminary work—listening to the melody, humming it through, then singing a stanza or two—try a little antiphonal singing. Have one group sing the first three phrases, another the next three and all join on the final phrase. Be sure to have everyone stand when singing the last stanza which is pure praise.

O Lord of Life

It seems rather fitting that the tune for this hymn, which speaks about the dead and is placed under the general heading "Commemoration" in the *Service Book and Hymnal,* should also be the tune for the Easter hymn "Good Christian men, rejoice and sing" (SBH 109). The joyous alleluias in both hymns truly express the old Hebrew meaning, "Praise Jehovah."

Hymns by Americans are not many in present-day hymnals. Are there reasons for this? Are American Christians not writing hymns? Frederick Hosmer was an American (d. 1929), and one of our most gifted hymnists. Like Samuel Longfellow and Samuel Johnson, he was a New England liberal, a product of the Harvard Divinity School. Perhaps this accounts for the infrequent references to Christ in his hymns. Note that Christ is not mentioned in this hymn. Yet, this is also true of the psalms, and we still use them in our worship. This hymn is truly a "psalm of grateful trust."

In teaching this hymn, use a fast tempo. Try beating one slow beat to each measure. It is always easier to slow down later. Be careful with the rhythm in measure seven and again in measure eleven. It might be interesting to point out the exact imitation of the melody in the first and second "alleluia," the second being a fourth lower, also that each of the three alleluias is sung at a lower pitch than the preceding one. For emphasis, shouldn't the next one be at a higher pitch? Can the climax be at a lower pitch?

Because this hymn is in a somewhat low range, it might be well to pitch it a tone higher for children.

This hymn can be used on many occasions. It is especially fitting for the last Sundays in the Trinity season, for All Saints' Day (or Sunday), and at Christian funerals. An especially stirring organ setting° on this tune has been written by Healey Willan.

°See appendix.

O Happy Day

To introduce this hymn, play side 6, band 7, of *A Time for Singing.** Discuss with the students what they have just heard. What is the mood of the music? Why is it joyful? Have the instrumentalists (organ and piccolo) caught the spirit of the text? Should they rather have introduced this hymn in a heavy, ponderous way? Why was the piccolo better for this hymn than a trumpet or an oboe?

Play the first few phrases of the hymn on a keyboard instrument in a very slow tempo and softly. Does the mood change? The notes are the same but by varying the tempo and the volume a change takes place.

Now that you have established the importance of musical mood, solicit ideas from the students concerning the way music can be used to intensify the mood of the words. Have the students sing the melody using "do" for each note instead of the words. When you have succeeded in invigorating the group to respond with a buoyant, joyful sound, sing the words.

But wait! Some of the words may need explanation. Do the students understand celestial, surcease, surge, ransomed? With small children, it may not be necessary to explain every word—some words are too difficult for them to understand anyway—but with older children they can be explained.

"O happy day" is from Norway. Wilhelm Andreas Wexels was appointed catechist of Our Savior's Church in Oslo in 1818, and 28 years later the pastor of this church which is the Cathedral church of Oslo. He continued as pastor of this church until his death in 1866. This was during a very trying time in the history of the church in Norway, and Wexels' ministry strongly influenced the return to conservative Lutheran theology.

This hymn could easily provide the introduction to a discussion about music appropriate to Christian funerals. Could this hymn be sung at a funeral? In fact, should the congregation sing hymns at funerals? The message of Christian victory over death is clearly proclaimed! As we use music to intensify the words, may we also witness to our victorious faith!

---

*See appendix.

Wake, Awake

Motivation

This is one of the theme songs, perhaps the principal one of the season of Advent. As such it deals with the coming of Christ, especially his second coming.

It is based on Matthew 25, The Ten Virgins, and Revelation 19, both Advent texts and appropriate to those themes.

Both text and tune were written by Philipp Nicolai, a German Lutheran pastor who saw many of his people die from pestilence and was moved to reflect on the last things. Remarkably, Nicolai was also author and composer of the chorale *Wie schön leuchtet* (How brightly beams the morning star), both of such intrinsic worth that they have been dubbed respectively the king and queen of chorales.

Presentation

The chorale appears in this arrangement as the closing chorus of J. S. Bach's cantata *Wachet auf*, composed for the Last Sunday after Trinity, 1731.

The second tune in the *Service Book and Hymnal* is especially suitable for the choir, a fact attested to by the continual movement of the inner voices. It should be presented by the choir, either in unison—the children's choir could be used—or in parts. It should be sung deliberately enough so that the moving voices do not sound hurried nor too slow. (The first tune in the *Service Book and Hymnal* is better for congregational singing.)

Application

1. Use in Sunday service on the Last Sunday after Trinity or the Second Sunday in Advent.

2. Base the organ prelude* on it, possibly also the postlude.

3. Use an anthem* based on this tune.

---

*See appendix.

4. Sing the second tune as an alternate stanza with the choir (alternatim), the congregation singing the other stanzas to the first tune. The choir can sing in parts. Or use the unison children's choir with instruments playing other parts.

5. Use an instrument such as a trumpet on the melody with the congregation, or with the organ in prelude or postlude.

6. Use as an Advent hymn in a hymn program devoted to the church year.

A Mighty Fortress Is Our God

There is a great deal in this hymn to captivate the imagination of children in the upper grades and junior high. At this age the tune should already be familiar, so one can dwell on other aspects of the hymn in teaching it.

Ask the class first of all to notice the author of the text. Ask what they know about him. Ask if anyone knows what the "tr." means in front of the name below Luther's. What was the original language and why? You can mention Luther's emphasis on vernacular language and congregational participation. Call attention to the fact that this hymn is based on Psalm 46. Make the children aware that information about the source of the text is found after the last stanza of each hymn. You might have them turn to several others to find this information.

Ask if they know who wrote the tune. Ask the name of the tune. Pronounce and explain it for them. Explain that every hymn tune has a name, which is always given in the upper left corner above the hymn, and the composer or source of the tune is in the upper right corner.

This hymn was a kind of battle cry of the Protestant Reformation. It is the only hymn by Luther which is used by almost all denominations. Surely this typically Lutheran hymn should be known and sung best by Lutherans.

Have them sing the first stanza. Ask who is in power at the end of the first stanza. Point out that the second half of the first stanza speaks of the power of the devil. Have them sing the first stanza again, thinking more carefully about the text. Ask them to sing stanza two and notice how it answers stanza one. Explain the meaning of "Sabaoth." Have them stand and sing the entire hymn. Congregations should always stand when this hymn is sung.

For All the Saints

Listen to these words: saints (not the ones who sit playing harps, but those like Luther who fought against many odds), rock, fortress, might, soldiers, true, bold, Captain, fight, glorious day, triumphant, win, victor, glory, fierce, warfare, struggle. To sing this hymn you need a vision of all that long procession of soldiers of the faith, following the Lord who triumphed over sin, death, and the devil. You need to fall in step behind them, joining in the march.

When you have caught this vision, throw yourself into the singing with abandon and openness. First, sing a nice big chord—D, G, B, D. Now sing the first line of the hymn. Do you recognize those notes from the chord? Do you feel the openness of it? After the fanfare of the first two measures we march along scalewise for three measures. But our excitement and enthusiasm cannot be contained for long, and our melody flares out in another bugle call: "Thy name, O Jesus, be forever blest. Alleluia!"

Be careful not to get out of step! We'll sing the first stanza through once, paying special attention to the words that fall on the accented notes, the first and third beats. A good, big bass note starts us off. In the next stanzas you will notice that some of the notes have no words and some have too many. Let those first and third beats be your guides. Put the word with the note above it, and keep those accents strong. This is one hymn that the organist has to sing along with if the accompaniment is to be helpful and meaningful. No fair taking liberties with the time! When the syllable falls on the down beat, *sing* it there, good and strong, for instance in the second measure of the second line.

Congregations can easily lose their way if no one points out how the stanzas are numbered. If a trumpeter is available use him on stanzas 1, 2, 3, 7, and 8. The choir could sing one or more of the four-part stanzas, and a brass quartet would be wonderful.

Leo Sowerby has written an organ prelude* on this tune which was given the name *Sine nomine* which means "without a name!"

---

*See appendix.

Appendix

Materials based on Hymns

Preludes
Free Harmonizations
Instrumental Accompaniments
Anthems
Descants

Code	Source	Publisher	Page
A MIGHTY FORTRESS IS OUR GOD (EIN' FESTE BURG)—SBH 150			
11-822	A Mighty Fortress (organ)—Arr., D. N. Johnson	APH	—
11-9495	Free Organ Accompaniments to Festival Hymns, vol. I—compilation	APH	26
11-1441	A Mighty Fortress Is Our God (choir, congregation, organ and optional trumpets) —Arr., D. N. Johnson	APH	—
AH, HOLY JESUS (HERZLIEBSTER JESU)—SBH 85			
11-9209	Hymntune Sketches for Beginning Organists—R. A. Nelson	APH	4
11-9295	Music for Worship with Easy Pedals—D. N. Johnson	APH	22
97-1151	Parish Organist, pt. 2—Fleischer, ed.	CPH	13
97-1403	Parish Organist, pt. 7—Goldschmidt, ed.	CPH	10
EP 4850	Twenty-five Chorale Preludes, bk. I—Walcha	CFP	22
11-1134	Ah, Holy Jesu (SSAB)—Cruger-Nelson	APH	—
11-1236	Ah, Holy Jesus (SSA)—Crueger-Malmin	APH	—
11-1198	Ah, Holy Jesus (SSAATTBB)—Crueger-Raphael	APH	—
11-9181	Festival Hymns with Descants—Arr., M. Pooler	APH	20
ALL GLORY BE TO GOD ON HIGH (ALLEN GOTT IN DER HÖH)—SBH 132			
—	Church Organist's Golden Treasury, vol. I—Pfatteicher-Davison	Pr	21
97-1145	Parish Organist, pt. 1—Fleischer ed.	CPH	7
97-1404	Parish Organist, pt. 8—Goldschmidt, ed.	CPH	48

7466	Seven Classic Preludes on Old Chorales—Edmundson	JF	3
—	Seventy-nine Chorales—Dupré	HWG	5
97-4554	Ten Chorale Improvisations, Op. 5, Set I—Manz	CPH	4
97-1370	Wedding Music, vol. II—compilation	CPH	4
11-9190	Free Harmonizations of Twelve Hymn Tunes—D. N. Johnson	APH	26
11-9305	Organ and Trumpet Accompaniments to Festival Hymns for Congregational Singing—Mudde	APH	2
11-1391	All Glory Be to God on High (SAB)—Arr., Johns	APH	—

ALL GLORY, LAUD, AND HONOR (ST. THEODULPH) (VALET WILL ICH DIR GEBEN—SBH 74

11-9206	Hymntune Preludes for the Organ, vol. II—Cassler	APH	8
11-9266	Liturgical Chorale Book (Preludes)—Leupold	APH	4
11-9495	Free Organ Accompaniments to Festival Hymns, vol. I—compilation	APH	50
11-9180	Free Organ Accompaniments to Hymns, vol. III—compilation	APH	15
—	All Glory Laud and Honor (brass)—Arr., R. Purvis	Lds	—
11-9201	Hymns for Brass, Set I—Arr., M. Johnson	APH	—

ALL PEOPLE THAT ON EARTH DO DWELL (OLD HUNDREDTH)—SBH 169

11-835	Triptych (organ)—Piet Post	APH	3
11-9185	Free Hymn Accompaniments for Manuals, bk. I—D. N. Johnson	APH	31
11-9495	Free Organ Accompaniments to Festival Hymns, vol. I—compilation	APH	46

ALL PRAISE TO THEE, ETERNAL LORD (TALLIS' CANON)—SBH 21

11-9190	Free Harmonizations of Twelve Hymn Tunes—D. N. Johnson	APH	42
11-9187	Free Organ Accompaniment to Hymns, vol. II—compilation	APH	15

ALLELUIA! JESUS LIVES (EASTER GLORY) (FRED TIL BOD)—SBH 100

11-9206	Hymntune Preludes for the Organ, vol. II—Cassler	APH	14

ALLELUIA, SONG OF SWEETNESS (TANTUM ERGO) (DULCE CARMEN)—SBH 58

11-9205	Hymntune Preludes for the Organ, vol. I—Cassler	APH	1
11-9321	Organ Music for the Church Year—Cassler	APH	70

BUILT ON A ROCK (KIRKEN)—SBH 151

11-9306	Organ Compositions, vol. I—F. M. Christiansen-Cassler	APH	48
11-9412	Six Chorale Improvisations for Organ—Hokanson	APH	4
11-9190	Free Harmonizations of Twelve Hymn Tunes—D. N. Johnson	APH	20
11-1416	Built on a Rock (SAB)—Lindeman-Brandon	APH	—
11-1322	Built on a Rock the Church Doth Stand (SATB & congregation)—Lindeman-Nystedt	APH	—
11-104	Built on the Rock (SSATTBB)—Lindeman-Christiansen	APH	—

CHILDREN OF THE HEAVENLY FATHER (SANDELL) TRYGGARE KAN INGEN VARA—SBH 572

11-9209	Hymntune Sketches for Beginning Organists—R. A. Nelson	APH	11
11-9384	Seven Improvisations on Hymns and Folk Tunes—Hokanson	APH	15
11-1019	Children of the Heavenly Father (SSAATB)—Arr., Myrvik	APH	—
11-9518	Unison Hymns with Descants—Arr., M. Pooler	APH	25

CHRIST JESUS LAY IN DEATH'S STRONG BANDS (CHRIST LAG IN TODESBANDEN)—SBH 98

11-9206	Hymntune Preludes for the Organ, vol. II—Cassler	APH	15
11-9321	Organ Music for the Church Year—Cassler	APH	41

COME, HOLY SPIRIT, GOD AND LORD (KOMM HEILIGER GEIST, HERRE GOTT)—SBH 122

11-9495	Free Organ Accompaniments to Festival Hymns, vol. I—compilation	APH	54
11-1431	Come, Holy Spirit, God and Lord (Unison or SATB)—Arr., Pasquet	APH	—

COMFORT, COMFORT YE MY PEOPLE (PSALM 42) (FREU DICH SEHR)—SBH 12

11-9205	Hymntune Preludes for the Organ, vol. I—Cassler	APH	6
11-9206	Hymntune Preludes for the Organ, vol. II—Cassler	APH	6
11-9295	Music for Worship with Easy Pedals—D. N. Johnson	APH	5
11-9187	Free Organ Accompaniment to Hymns, vol. II—compilation	APH	5

CROWN HIM WITH MANY CROWNS (DIADEMATA)—SBH 431

11-9093 Crown Him with Many Crowns (choir, congregation, organ & trumpets)—Arr., Pelz — APH

DECK THYSELF WITH JOY AND GLADNESS (SCHMÜCKE DICH)—SBH 262

11-830	Deck Thyself with Joy and Gladness (organ)—Handel-Owen	APH	2
11-9208	Hymntune Preludes for the Organ, vol. IV—Cassler	APH	52
97-1154	Parish Organist, pt. 3—Fleischer, ed.	CPH	30
11-9186	Free Hymn Accompaniments for Manuals, bk. II—D. N. Johnson	APH	
1896	Deck Thyself with Joy and Gladness (SATB)—Handel-Ehret	Pro	

FOR ALL THE SAINTS (SINE NOMINE)—SBH 144

819	Prelude on "Sine Nomine"—Sowerby	HWG	1
11-9190	Free Harmonizations of Twelve Hymn Tunes—D. N. Johnson	APH	9
11-9181	Eight Descants—Arr., Cartford	APH	

FROM HEAVEN ABOVE TO EARTH I COME (VOM HIMMEL HOCH)—SBH 22

11-801	From Heaven Above to Earth I Come (organ)—Arr., Mudde	APH	31
11-9307	Organ Compositions, vol. II—F. M. Christiansen-Cassler	APH	52
11-9495	Free Organ Accompaniments to Festival Hymns, vol. I—compilation	APH	
11-1471	From Heaven Above (SSATB)—Schein-Riedel	APH	
11-101	From Heaven Above (SSAATTBB)—Schumann-Christiansen	APH	

GOD'S WORD IS OUR GREAT HERITAGE (EIN' FESTE BURG)—SBH 257

| 11-822 | A Mighty Fortress (organ)—Arr., D. N. Johnson | APH | 26 |
| 11-9495 | Free Organ Accompaniments to Festival Hymns, vol. I—compilation | APH | |

HOLY GOD, WE PRAISE THY NAME (TE DEUM) (GROSSER GOTT)—SBH 167

11-9202 Holy God, We Praise Thy Name (choir, congregation, organ & trumpets)—Arr., Pelz — APH

HOW BRIGHTLY BEAMS THE MORNING STAR (WIE SCHÖN LEUCHTET)—SBH 404

11-9266 Liturgical Chorale Book (Preludes)—Leupold — APH — 24

104

11-9321 Organ Music for the Church Year—Cassler — APH 24
11-9495 Free Organ Accompaniments to Festival Hymns, vol. I—compilation — APH 33
11-9305 Organ and Trumpet Accompaniments to Festival Hymns for Congregational Singing—Arr., Mudde — APH 13

IMMORTAL, INVISIBLE, GOD ONLY WISE (ST. DENIO)—SBH 172
11-9207 Hymntune Preludes for the Organ, vol. III—Cassler — APH 23
11-9495 Free Organ Accompaniments to Festival Hymns, vol. I—compilation — APH 22
11-1440 Immortal, Invisible, God Only Wise (SAB)—Arr., Leupold — APH —
11-9518 Unison Hymns with Descants—Arr., M. Pooler — APH 18

JESUS, NAME ALL NAMES ABOVE (WERDE MUNTER)—SBH 67
11-9206 Hymntune Preludes for the Organ, vol. II—Cassler — APH 4
11-1319 Jesus, Name All Names Above (SA)—Schop-Bach-M. Pooler — APH —

JESUS, PRICELESS TREASURE (JESU, MEINE FREUDE)—SBH 575
11-9207 Hymntune Preludes for the Organ, vol. III—Cassler — APH 22
11-9266 Liturgical Chorale Book (Preludes)—Leupold — APH 1
— Liturgical Year, The—Bach — Pr 33
97-1370 Wedding Music, vol. II—compilation — CPH 20
11-1041 Jesu, Priceless Treasure (SATB)—Bach — APH —

JESUS SHALL REIGN (DUKE STREET)—SBH 307
11-9190 Free Harmonizations of Twelve Hymn Tunes—D. N. Johnson — APH 6
— Great Hymns with Descants—Arr., Mead — SHM 27

JESUS, THOU JOY OF LOVING HEARTS (WALTON) (GERMANY)—SBH 483
7466 Seven Classic Preludes on Old Chorales—Edmundson — JF 22
11-9186 Free Hymn Accompaniments for Manuals, bk. II—D. N. Johnson — APH 52

LET ALL MORTAL FLESH KEEP SILENCE (PICARDY)—SBH 281
11-9208 Hymntune Preludes for the Organ, vol. IV—Cassler — APH 1
11-9209 Hymntune Sketches for Beginning Organists—R. A. Nelson — APH 8

11-1161	Let All Mortal Flesh Keep Silence (SATB)—Arr., F. M. and P. Christiansen	APH	—
2014	Let All Mortal Flesh Keep Silence (SATB)—Arr., Clokey	CPH	—
2142	Let All Mortal Flesh Keep Silence (SATB)—Arr., Darst	HWG	—
5	Let All Mortal Flesh Keep Silence (SATB)—Arr., Holst	Gal	—
8009	Let All Mortal Flesh Keep Silence (SATB)—Arr., Sateren	SHM	—

LIFT UP YOUR HEADS, YE MIGHTY GATES (TRURO)—SBH 8

11-9205	Hymntune Preludes for the Organ, vol. I—Cassler	APH	7
11-9190	Free Harmonizations of Twelve Hymn Tunes—D. N. Johnson	APH	12
11-1109	Lift Up Your Heads (SATB)—Arr., C. W. Andersen	APH	—
11-9518	Unison Hymns with Descants—Arr., M. Pooler	APH	5

LOOK YE SAINTS, THE SIGHT IS GLORIOUS (BRYN CALFARIA)—SBH 114

| — | Three Preludes on Welsh Hymn Tunes—Vaughan Williams | Gal | 2 |
| 11-9155 | Eight Descants—Arr., Cartford | APH | 15 |

LORD JESUS CHRIST, BE PRESENT NOW (HERR JESU CHRIST, DICH ZU UNS WEND)—SBH 188

—	Church Organist's Golden Treasury, vol. II—Pfatteicher-Davison	Pr	24
97-1151	Parish Organist, pt. 2—Fleischer, ed.	CPH	7
11-804	Lord Jesus Christ, Be Present Now (organ)—Guenter-Raphael	APH	—

LORD, KEEP US STEADFAST IN THY WORD (ERHALT UNS, HERR)—SBH 155

11-9207	Hymntune Preludes for the Organ, vol. III—Cassler	APH	14
11-9266	Liturgical Chorale Book (Preludes)—Leupold	APH	47
11-1448	Lord, Keep Us Steadfast (SAB)—Arr., Distler	APH	—
11-1401	Lord, Keep Us Steadfast (SSA)—Luther-Kenneth Jennings	APH	—
11-1394	Lord, Keep Us Steadfast (SAB)—Arr., Johns	APH	—
11-1352	Lord, Keep Us Steadfast (SATB)—Walter-Wunderlich	APH	—

LOVE DIVINE, ALL LOVES EXCELLING (HYFRYDOL)—SBH 397

| — | Three Preludes on Welsh Hymn Tunes—Vaughan Williams | Gal | 10 |
| 11-9186 | Free Hymn Accompaniments for Manuals, bk. II—D. N. Johnson | APH | 5 |

11-9495	Free Organ Accompaniments to Festival Hymns, vol. I—compilation	APH	10
11-9155	Eight Descants—Arr., Cartford	APH	5

MY GOD, HOW WONDERFUL THOU ART (DUNDEE) (FRENCH)—SBH 181

11-9306	Organ Compositions, vol. I—F. M. Christiansen-Cassler	APH	7
11-9186	Free Hymn Accompaniments for Manuals, bk. II—D. N. Johnson	APH	12
11-9201	Hymns for Brass, Set I—Arr., M. Johnson	APH	—
11-178	My God, How Wonderful (SSAATTBB)—Arr., F. M. Christiansen	APH	—
11-M15	My God! How Wonderful (SA)—Arr., Malmin	APH	—
11-1097	My God, How Wonderful (S) (SATB)—Arr., Overby	APH	—

MY SONG IS LOVE UNKNOWN (RHOSYMEDRE)—SBH 65

—	Three Preludes on Welsh Hymn Tunes—Vaughan Williams	Gal	6
11-9180	Free Organ Accompaniments to Hymns, vol. III—compilation	APH	8

O BREAD OF LIFE (INNSBRUCK)—SBH 271

11-9412	Six Chorale Improvisations for Organ—Hokanson	APH	6
11-103	O Bread of Life (SATB)—Isaac-Christiansen	APH	—

O COME, O COME, EMMANUEL (VENI, VENI, EMMANUEL)—SBH 2

11-9221	Organ Music for the Church Year—Cassler	APH	14
11-1085	O Come, O Come, Emmanuel (SATB)—Arr., P. Christiansen	APH	—
11-1395	O Come, O Come, Emmanuel (SAB)—Arr., Johns	APH	—

O GOD, ETERNAL SOURCE OF LOVE (DARMSTADT) (O GOTT, DU FROMMER GOTT)—SBH 460

11-9186	Free Hymn Accompaniments for Manuals, bk. II—D. N. Johnson	APH	10

O HAPPY DAY (LOBT GOTT, IHR CHRISTEN)—SBH 197

11-9186	Free Hymn Accompaniments for Manuals, bk. II—D. N. Johnson	APH	15
11-9505	Organ and Trumpet Accompaniments to Festival Hymns for Congregational Singing—Mudde	APH	12

O HOW SHALL I RECEIVE THEE (ST. THEODULPH) (VALET WILL ICH DIR GEBEN)—SBH 11

No.	Title	Pub.	
—	All Glory Laud and Honor (brass)—Arr., R. Purvis	Lds	—
11-9206	Hymntune Preludes for the Organ, vol. II—Cassler	APH	8
11-9266	Liturgical Chorale Book (Preludes)—Leupold	APH	4
31.182	Seasonal Chorale Preludes for Manuals Only, bk. I—Trevor	Oxf	24
11-9495	Free Organ Accompaniments to Festival Hymns, vol. I—compilation	APH	50
11-9180	Free Organ Accompaniments to Hymns, vol. III—compilation	APH	15
11-9305	Organ and Trumpet Accompaniments to Festival Hymns for Congregational Singing—Mudde	APH	3
11-9201	Hymns for Brass, Set I—Arr., M. Johnson	APH	—

O LAMB OF GOD (O LAMM GOTTES)—SBH 70

No.	Title	Pub.	
—	Liturgical Year, The—Bach	Pr	61
11-9306	Organ Compositions, vol. I—F. M. Christiansen-Cassler	APH	4
97-1403	Parish Organist—pt. 7—Goldschmidt, ed.	CPH	14
11-9186	Free Hymn Accompaniments for Manuals, bk. II—D. N. Johnson	APH	24
11-133	Lamb of God (SATB)—Arr., F. M. Christiansen	APH	—
11-1317	O Lamb of God Most Holy (SATB)—Decius-Running	APH	—

O LORD OF LIFE (VULPIUS) (GELOBT SEI GOTT)—SBH 600

No.	Title	Pub.	
11-9295	Music for Worship with Easy Pedals—D. N. Johnson	APH	29
97-3903	Six Chorale Preludes, Set I—Willan	CPH	10
11-9190	Free Harmonizations of Twelve Hymn Tunes—D. N. Johnson	APH	36
11-9201	Hymns for Brass, Set I—Arr., M. Johnson	APH	—
11-9518	Unison Hymns with Descants—Arr., M. Pooler	APH	22

O SACRED HEAD NOW WOUNDED (PASSION CHORALE)—SBH 88

No.	Title	Pub.	
11-9206	Hymntune Preludes for the Organ, vol. II—Cassler	APH	13
11-9306	Organ Compositions, vol. I—F. M. Christiansen-Cassler	APH	42
11-817	Prelude on "O Sacred Head"—Boeringer	APH	—

OF THE FATHER'S LOVE BEGOTTEN (DIVINUM MYSTERIUM) (CORDE NATUS EX PARENTIS)—SBH 17

| 11-9321 | Organ Music for the Church Year—Cassler | APH | 19 |
| 11-9190 | Free Harmonizations of Twelve Hymn Tunes—D. N. Johnson | APH | 40 |

OPEN NOW THY GATES OF BEAUTY (NEANDER) (UNSER HERRSCHER)—SBH 187

| 97-1151 | Parish Organist, pt. 2—Fleischer, ed. | CPH | 54 |
| 97-4454 | Ten Chorale Improvisations, op. 5, Set I—Manz | CPH | 14 |

OUR GOD, TO WHOM WE TURN (DARMSTADT)—SBH 171

| 11-9186 | Free Hymn Accompaniments for Manuals, bk. II—D. N. Johnson | APH | 10 |

OUT OF THE DEPTHS I CRY TO THEE (AUS TIEFER NOT)—SBH 372

| 11-9266 | Liturgical Chorale Book (Preludes)—Leupold | APH | 42 |

PRAISE TO THE LORD (LOBE DEN HERREN)—SBH 408

11-9307	Organ Compositions, vol. II—F. M. Christiansen-Cassler	APH	17
11-9185	Free Hymn Accompaniments for Manuals, bk. I—D. N. Johnson	APH	15
11-9495	Free Organ Accompaniments to Festival Hymns, vol. I—compilation	APH	4
11-9305	Organ and Trumpet Accompaniments to Festival Hymns for Congregational Singing—Mudde	APH	14
11-76	Praise to the Lord (SSAATTBB)—Arr., F. M. Christiansen	APH	—
11-9155	Eight Descants—Arr., Cartford	APH	13

THAT EASTER DAY WITH JOY WAS BRIGHT (PUER NOBIS)—SBH 94

| 11-9186 | Free Hymn Accompaniments for Manuals, bk. II—D. N. Johnson | APH | 18 |

THE KING OF LOVE MY SHEPHERD IS (ST. COLUMBA)—SBH 530

| 11-9207 | Hymntune Preludes for the Organ, vol. III—Cassler | APH | 16 |

TURN BACK, O MAN (OLD 124TH)—SBH 348

| 11-9186 | Free Hymn Accompaniments for Manuals, bk. II—D. N. Johnson | APH | 36 |
| 6 | Turn Back, O Man (SATB)—Arr., Holst | Gal | — |

WAKE, AWAKE (WACHET AUF) —SBH 7

11-9209	Hymntune Sketches for Beginning Organists—R. A. Nelson	APH	1
11-9266	Liturgical Chorale Book (Preludes)—Leupold	APH	32
—	Lutheran Organist, The—Holler, ed.	HWG	4
97-1157	Parish Organist, pt. 4—Fleischer, ed.	CPH	14
—	Seventy-nine Chorales—Dupré	HWG	86
97-4554	Ten Chorale Improvisations, op. 5, Set I—Manz	CPH	20
11-9190	Free Harmonizations of Twelve Hymn Tunes—D. N. Johnson	APH	34
11-1320	Wake, Awake (SATB)—Nicolai-Bach	APH	—
11-102	Wake, Awake (SSAATTBB)—Nicolai-Christiansen	APH	—

YE WATCHERS AND YE HOLY ONES (LASST UNS ERFREUEN)—SBH 437

11-9295	Music for Worship with Easy Pedals—D. N. Johnson	APH	24
11-9412	Six Chorale Improvisations for Organ—Hokanson	APH	13
11-9190	Free Harmonizations of Twelve Hymn Tunes—D. N. Johnson	APH	16
11-1240	Ye Watchers and Ye Holy Ones (SATB)—Arr., Cassler	APH	—
11-9155	Eight Descants—Arr., Cartford	APH	3

32-941   A Time for Singing

62 Hymns from the *Hymn of the Week Songbook*
Choral group directed by Dale Warland,
accompanied by Paul Manz at the organ.

Three 12", 33⅓ rpm records, compatible sound. May
be played on monaural or stereo record player.

11-9195   A Guide to Music for the Church Year

An extensive list of anthems and organ music for the
Sundays and festivals of the church year. Anthem
texts quote or relate to the Lessons and Propers for
the day. Organ selections are chorale preludes based
on related hymn texts.

Key to Publishers

APH	Augsburg Publishing House
CFP	C. F. Peeters
CPH	Concordia Publishing House
Gal	Galaxy
HWG	H. W. Gray
JF	J. Fischer
Lds	Leeds Publishing Co.
Oxf	Oxford
Pr	Presser
Pro	Pro Art
SHM	Schmitt, Hall & McCreary